Best of
GREAT AMERICAN
Comforts made simple

GARDEN *of* **GRAPES.**

Printed in the United States of America

Published by Garden of Grapes

First Edition: 2023

Library of Congress Cataloging-in-Publication Data

Printed on acid-free paper.

Introduction

Welcome to "Best of Great American Comforts Made Simple: 100+ Easy Comfort Regional American Recipes to Cook at Home." In the following pages, we embark on a culinary journey that celebrates the heart and soul of American comfort food. This cookbook is an ode to the flavors that have graced American tables for generations, inviting you to explore the rich tapestry of regional cuisine from coast to coast.

The central theme of this cookbook is rooted in the idea of simplicity and comfort. We believe that great American comforts should be accessible to all, and this book is designed to make that a reality. Our inspiration for creating this collection of recipes comes from a deep appreciation for the diverse culinary traditions that define our nation. Each dish featured in this book captures the essence of a particular American region, from the warm and soul-soothing Southern classics to the hearty and satisfying Midwestern fare.

Our goal is to bring the warmth and familiarity of these regional favorites into your home kitchen. Through easy-to-follow instructions, helpful tips, and a passion for simplifying the cooking process, we aim to empower you to recreate these beloved recipes with ease. Whether you are an experienced home cook or just starting your culinary journey, there's something here for everyone.

Within the pages of this cookbook, you can expect to find a carefully curated selection of over 100 recipes that showcase the best of American comfort food. From savory dishes that warm the heart to sweet treats that evoke memories of simpler times, we've included a diverse range of recipes to satisfy all tastes. Each recipe has been crafted with precision and love, ensuring that you can bring the flavors of regional America to your table with confidence.

"Best of Great American Comforts Made Simple" is more than just a cookbook; it's an invitation to experience the comfort and joy of American regional cuisine in the comfort of your own home. We hope that these recipes not only fill your kitchen with delightful aromas but also create lasting memories with family and friends. So, without further ado, let's embark on this delicious journey together and discover the timeless comforts that regional American cooking has to offer.

Cajun Jambalaya
See page, 71

Cooking Philosophy or Approach

The approach to cooking and food within the pages of this cookbook is rooted in the belief that simplicity and comfort are at the heart of great American cuisine. The recipes featured here are a testament to the idea that delicious food doesn't need to be complicated or intimidating. Instead, it should be approachable and enjoyable for cooks of all levels.

Our philosophy is to celebrate the inherent flavors of quality ingredients and let them shine. We believe in the magic of using fresh, locally sourced ingredients whenever possible, allowing their natural goodness to take center stage. In doing so, we pay homage to the diversity of American agriculture and the unique flavors that each region contributes to the culinary landscape.

While the recipes in this cookbook span a wide range of American regional cuisine, they all share a common thread of simplicity and accessibility. Whether you're making a classic Southern comfort dish or trying your hand at a hearty New England favorite, you'll find that the instructions are clear, concise, and designed to make your cooking experience enjoyable.

Throughout the book, you'll also find tips and techniques that aim to demystify any potentially tricky aspects of cooking. From mastering the art of creating flaky pie crusts to achieving the perfect balance of spices in a Cajun-inspired dish, we're here to guide you every step of the way.

Additionally, we encourage creativity and adaptation. While we provide tried-and-true recipes, we also invite you to make them your own. Feel free to experiment with ingredients, adjust flavors to suit your palate, and add your personal touch to each dish. Cooking, after all, is not just about following a set of instructions; it's about expressing yourself through the food you prepare and share with loved ones.

This cookbook embodies an approach to cooking that values simplicity, celebrates the diversity of American regional cuisine, and empowers you to become a confident and creative home cook. So, let's roll up our sleeves, don our aprons, and embark on a culinary adventure that's as delicious as it is satisfying. Happy cooking!

Tips for Successful Cooking

Certainly, here are some valuable tips to ensure your cooking endeavors are successful while using the recipes in this cookbook:

Preparation is Key: Before you begin cooking, take the time to read through the entire recipe. Familiarize yourself with the ingredients and steps involved. This not only helps you understand the process but also ensures you have all the necessary ingredients on hand.

Fresh Ingredients Matter: Whenever possible, opt for fresh, high-quality ingredients. The flavor and texture of your final dish will greatly benefit from using fresh produce, meats, and dairy products.

Proper Measuring: Accuracy in measuring ingredients is crucial, especially in baking. Invest in reliable measuring cups and spoons, and level off dry ingredients to ensure consistent results.

Room Temperature Ingredients: For many recipes, particularly in baking, ingredients like eggs, butter, and dairy products are best used at room temperature. This ensures they incorporate smoothly into the mixture.

Knife Skills: Develop good knife skills for efficient and safe chopping, dicing, and slicing. A sharp knife is not only safer but also makes your prep work more enjoyable.

Balancing Flavors: Taste as you go and adjust seasonings as needed. Achieving the right balance of salt, acidity, sweetness, and heat is often the key to a successful dish.

Don't Rush Browning: When searing or browning ingredients, give them time to develop flavor and color. Crowding the pan can lead to steaming instead of browning, so work in batches if necessary.

Patience with Baking: Baking requires precision. Invest in an oven thermometer to ensure your oven is at the correct temperature. Avoid opening the oven door too often, as this can affect baking times and results.

Rest and Relax: Allow dishes like roasted meats or baked goods to rest before serving. This allows flavors to meld, juices to redistribute, and ensures a more enjoyable eating experience.

Clean as You Go: Keep your workspace organized and clean as you cook. This not only makes the process smoother but also reduces the post-cooking cleanup.

Experiment and Adapt: While recipes provide guidelines, feel free to adapt them to suit your taste preferences. Cooking is an art, and adding your personal touch can make a dish truly yours.

Have Fun: Cooking should be an enjoyable experience. Don't be afraid to make mistakes; they can be valuable learning opportunities. Embrace the joy of creating delicious meals for yourself and loved ones.

By incorporating these tips into your cooking routine, you'll not only have a smoother experience with the recipes in this cookbook but also become a more confident and skilled home cook. Happy cooking!

Kitchen Essentials

Certainly, here's a list of essential kitchen tools and equipment that you'll find useful when preparing the recipes in this cookbook, along with some tips on how to use them effectively:

1. Chef's Knife: Invest in a high-quality chef's knife. It's the workhorse of the kitchen and essential for chopping, slicing, and dicing. Keep it sharp for safe and efficient cutting.

2. Cutting Board: Use a sturdy cutting board made of wood or plastic. Wooden boards are gentle on knife blades, while plastic boards are easy to clean and sanitize.

3. Measuring Cups and Spoons: Accurate measurement is key, especially in baking. Invest in reliable measuring cups and spoons and level off dry ingredients for precise measurements.

4. Mixing Bowls: Have a variety of mixing bowls in different sizes for mixing ingredients, marinating, and more. Stainless steel or glass bowls are durable and easy to clean.

5. Whisk: Whisks come in various sizes and shapes. They're essential for mixing and incorporating ingredients smoothly, especially in baking and making sauces.

6. Wooden Spoon and Spatula: Wooden utensils are gentle on cookware and great for stirring, sautéing, and mixing. A spatula is handy for flipping and turning delicate items.

7. Pots and Pans: A set of quality pots and pans, including a skillet, saucepan, and stockpot, is essential for various cooking techniques. Non-stick options are great for easy cleanup.

8. Ovenproof Bakeware: Invest in baking sheets, cake pans, and casserole dishes for all your baking and roasting needs. Opt for non-stick or use parchment paper to prevent sticking.

9. Thermometer: A kitchen thermometer is crucial for accurately gauging the temperature of meats, baked goods, and liquids. This ensures perfectly cooked dishes.

10. Peeler: A vegetable peeler is useful for peeling and trimming vegetables and fruits quickly and efficiently.

11. Grater/Zester: Graters are handy for shredding cheese, vegetables, and more. A zester is excellent for adding citrus zest to dishes.

12. Can Opener: For opening canned ingredients or goods, a reliable can opener is a must.

13. Colander/Strainer: Use a colander or strainer for draining pasta, rinsing produce, and straining liquids from solids.

14. Food Processor or Blender: These appliances are versatile for chopping, pureeing, and blending ingredients for sauces, soups, and more.

15. Baking Supplies: Keep essentials like parchment paper, baking mats, and cooling racks on hand for baking success.

16. Timer: A kitchen timer helps you keep track of cooking times accurately, preventing overcooking or burning.

17. Tongs: Tongs are handy for flipping items in a hot pan, grilling, or serving.

18. Kitchen Scale: A kitchen scale is useful for precise measurement of ingredients, especially in baking.

19. Canisters/Storage Containers: Keep your pantry organized with airtight canisters or storage containers for dry goods like flour, sugar, and spices.

20. Silicone Oven Mitts: Protect your hands from heat with durable and heat-resistant oven mitts.

Using these essential kitchen tools effectively involves proper maintenance and safe handling. Regularly sharpen knives, clean equipment promptly after use, and store items in an organized manner for easy access. With the right tools at your disposal, you'll be well-prepared to tackle the delicious recipes in this cookbook with confidence. Happy cooking!

Buffalo Wings
See page, 74

Flavor Pairing Suggestions

Certainly, here are some flavor pairing suggestions to inspire your culinary creativity and help you experiment with complementary flavors and ingredients:

1. Sweet and Savory: The classic combination of sweet and savory is a winner. Try pairing honey with roasted vegetables, balsamic vinegar with strawberries, or figs with prosciutto for a delightful contrast of flavors.

2. Citrus and Herbs: Citrus fruits like lemon, lime, and orange pair beautifully with fresh herbs like basil, mint, and cilantro. These combinations add brightness and freshness to dishes like salads, marinades, and cocktails.

3. Spice and Heat: Spice up your dishes by combining different types of heat. For example, pair jalapeños with cooling yogurt, or use cayenne pepper to enhance the warmth of cinnamon in desserts.

4. Creamy and Crunchy: Achieve textural balance by combining creamy elements with crunchy ones. Think of creamy avocado with crispy bacon or a rich cheese sauce with toasted breadcrumbs.

5. Earthy and Nutty: Earthy flavors from mushrooms or roasted root vegetables can be complemented by nutty ingredients like toasted almonds, pine nuts, or sesame seeds. These combinations add depth and texture to your dishes.

6. Umami Boost: Enhance the savory umami flavor with ingredients like soy sauce, miso paste, or Parmesan cheese. These umami-rich elements can elevate a wide range of dishes, from stir-fries to soups.

7. Fruity and Spicy: Fruit can balance out spicy dishes beautifully. Try adding mango to a spicy curry or pineapple to a chili for a touch of sweetness and acidity.

8. Fresh and Tangy: Brighten up your meals with tangy ingredients like Greek yogurt, sour cream, or pickled vegetables. They work well with fresh herbs and citrus to create refreshing and zesty flavors.

9. Nutmeg and Greens: Nutmeg pairs wonderfully with leafy greens like spinach, kale, and Swiss chard. A sprinkle of freshly grated nutmeg can add warmth and depth to these vegetables.

10. Chocolate and Sea Salt: The combination of dark chocolate and a pinch of sea salt is a classic and indulgent pairing. Whether in desserts or as a finishing touch on a savory dish, it's a flavor contrast that's hard to resist.

11. Garlic and Lemon: This dynamic duo adds zing to a wide range of dishes. Garlic's earthy richness complements the bright acidity of lemon, creating a harmonious balance of flavors.

12. Fresh Berries and Cream: Berries like strawberries, raspberries, and blueberries shine when paired with whipped cream, yogurt, or custard. This classic dessert pairing is perfect for tarts, parfaits, and shortcakes.

These flavor pairing suggestions are just the beginning. Don't hesitate to experiment with different combinations to create your own unique dishes. Cooking is an art, and exploring the interplay of flavors is one of its most rewarding aspects. So, go ahead, mix and match, and discover exciting new tastes in your kitchen. Happy cooking and experimenting!

Table of contents

Chapter 1:
Eastern Delights

2 slices   350/serving   90 minutes

New York-style Pizza

Ingredients:

- 1 lb pizza dough
- 1/2 cup tomato sauce
- 2 cups shredded mozzarella
- Toppings of your choice: pepperoni, mushrooms, peppers, etc.
- Olive oil, for drizzling
- Salt and pepper, to taste

Substitutions

- Use a store-bought pizza crust for a quicker version.
- Experiment with different cheeses and unique toppings for a personal touch.
- For a crispy crust, preheat a pizza stone in the oven before baking.
- To add an authentic touch, sprinkle red pepper flakes for a little heat.

A slice of the Big Apple! This iconic pizza is the heart of New York City. Its origins trace back to Italian immigrants who brought their pizza-making artistry to the bustling streets. The thin crust, zesty tomato sauce, gooey mozzarella, and your favorite toppings create a symphony of flavors. Every bite is a taste of history and urban charm.

Directions

1. Preheat your oven to 475°F (245°C).
2. Roll out the pizza dough on a floured surface to your desired thickness.
3. Transfer the dough to a baking sheet.
4. Spread the tomato sauce evenly over the dough, leaving a border for the crust.
5. Sprinkle the shredded mozzarella over the sauce.
6. Add your selected toppings.
7. Drizzle with olive oil and season with salt and pepper.
8. Bake for 12-15 minutes or until the crust is golden and the cheese is bubbly.
9. Let cool slightly before slicing and savoring this New York masterpiece!

1 bowl

250/se rving

60 minutes

Clam Chowder

A creamy ode to Massachusetts' maritime heritage. The ocean's bounty meets hearty comfort in this chowder. Imagine tender clams, potatoes, and onions harmonizing in a velvety broth. It's a taste of coastal history, where every spoonful tells a story of seafaring New Englanders and their love for wholesome sustenance.

Ingredients:

- 2 dozen fresh clams, scrubbed and cleaned
- 3 slices bacon, chopped
- 1 onion, finely chopped
- 2 potatoes, diced
- 2 cups milk
- 1 cup heavy cream
- Salt and pepper, to taste
- Fresh parsley, chopped, for garnish

Directions

1. In a large pot, cook bacon over medium heat until crispy. Remove and set aside.
2. In the same pot, sauté chopped onion until translucent.
3. Add diced potatoes and just enough water to cover them. Simmer until potatoes are tender.
4. Add milk and clams (with juices). Cook until clams open.
5. Stir in heavy cream and cooked bacon. Simmer, but do not boil.
6. Season with salt and pepper.
7. Serve hot, garnished with chopped parsley.
8. Dive into the flavors of coastal Massachusetts!

Substitutions
- Swap fresh clams with canned clams if fresh aren't available.
- For a smoky twist, use smoked haddock instead of clams.
- Opt for vegetable stock for a lighter chowder.
- Add a pinch of thyme for extra depth of flavor.

1 roll | 320/se rving | 30 minutes

Lobster Roll

Maine's gift to the world: the luscious lobster roll. Sweet, succulent lobster meat tucked into a buttered and toasted bun. This seaside delight captures the essence of summer picnics and coastal escapes. With each bite, savor the indulgence and the simplicity of the ocean's finest treasure.

Ingredients:

- 1 lb cooked lobster meat, chopped
- 1/4 cup mayonnaise
- 2 celery stalks, finely chopped
- 1 tablespoon lemon juice
- Salt and pepper, to taste
- Buttered and toasted hot dog buns
- Fresh chives, chopped, for garnish

Directions

1. In a bowl, combine lobster meat, mayonnaise, chopped celery, and lemon juice.
2. Gently mix until well coated. Season with salt and pepper.
3. Chill the lobster mixture for at least 20 minutes.
4. Fill the toasted buns with the chilled lobster salad.
5. Garnish with chopped chives.
6. Serve with a side of coleslaw or potato chips.
7. Let the taste of Maine's coast transport you to a summer day by the sea!

Substitutions

- Replace lobster with crab meat for a crab roll.
- Use Greek yogurt instead of mayonnaise for a healthier twist.
- Add a dash of Old Bay seasoning for a classic New England flavor.
- Choose split-top buns for an authentic presentation.

1 slice

280/se rving

60 minutes

Boston Cream Pie

Ingredients:

- 1 1/2 cups all-purpose flour
- 1 1/2 teaspoons baking powder
- 1/4 teaspoon salt
- 1/2 cup unsalted butter, softened
- 1 cup granulated sugar
- 2 large eggs
- 1 teaspoon vanilla extract
- 1/2 cup whole milk
- 1 1/2 cups heavy cream
- 1/4 cup powdered sugar
- 1 teaspoon vanilla extract
- 4 oz semisweet chocolate, chopped
- 2 tablespoons unsalted butter

Substitutions

- Use instant vanilla pudding for a quicker custard.
- Dark chocolate can replace semisweet for a more intense chocolate flavor.
- Add sliced almonds on top of the chocolate glaze for a nutty touch.
- Incorporate a thin layer of raspberry jam for a fruity twist.

A cake with a tale: the Boston Cream Pie. Despite its name, it's not a pie at all! It's a classic dessert made of two fluffy cake layers cradling silky vanilla custard, all glazed in rich chocolate. Originating from Boston's Parker House Hotel, it's a confectionery legacy that bridges the gap between cake and custard. Indulge in history and taste the sweet side of Beantown.

Directions

1. Preheat oven to 350°F (175°C). Grease and flour two 9-inch round cake pans.
2. In a bowl, whisk flour, baking powder, and salt.
3. In another bowl, cream butter and granulated sugar until light and fluffy.
4. Beat in eggs, one at a time. Stir in vanilla.
5. Gradually add dry ingredients, alternating with milk. Mix until just combined.
6. Divide batter between pans. Bake for 25-30 minutes.
7. For custard, bring cream to a simmer. Whisk powdered sugar, vanilla, and cornstarch. Gradually whisk into simmering cream until thickened. Chill.
8. Spread custard on one cake layer. Top with the other layer.
9. For chocolate glaze, melt chocolate and butter. Pour over the cake.
10. Chill before serving. Savor the sweet history of Boston Cream Pie!

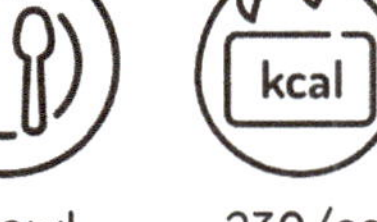
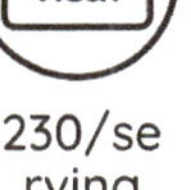

1 bowl

230/se
rving

45
minutes

Rhode Island Clam Chowder

Ingredients:

- 2 dozen little neck clams, scrubbed and cleaned
- 2 slices bacon, chopped
- 1 onion, finely chopped
- 2 potatoes, diced
- 2 carrots, diced
- 2 celery stalks, diced
- 4 cups chicken or vegetable broth
- 1 bay leaf
- Fresh thyme sprigs
- Salt and pepper, to taste
- Chopped fresh parsley, for garnish

Substitutions

- Use canned clams if fresh ones aren't available.
- Customize the vegetables with seasonal produce.
- Add a splash of white wine for an extra layer of flavor.
- Serve with oyster crackers for an authentic touch.

Rhode Island's own take on chowder! Unlike its creamier cousins, this clear broth chowder stars tender clams, potatoes, and a medley of fresh vegetables. It's a lighter way to enjoy the ocean's treasures while still savoring the coastal charm. Gather 'round and let the flavors of Rhode Island's shores dance on your taste buds.

Directions

1. In a pot, cook bacon over medium heat until crispy. Remove and set aside.
2. Sauté chopped onion until translucent.
3. Add diced potatoes, carrots, and celery. Sauté for a few minutes.
4. Pour in broth, add bay leaf and thyme. Simmer until vegetables are tender.
5. Add clams (with juices) and cooked bacon. Simmer until clams open.
6. Season with salt and pepper.
7. Ladle into bowls, garnish with chopped parsley.
8. Enjoy the clear and comforting flavors of Rhode Island!

1 taco

420/serving

45 minutes

Indian Taco

Ingredients:

- For Fry Bread:
  - 2 cups all-purpose flour
  - 2 teaspoons baking powder
  - 1/2 teaspoon salt
  - 1 cup warm water
  - Vegetable oil, for frying
- For Chili Topping:
  - 1 lb ground beef or bison
  - 1 onion, chopped
  - 2 cloves garlic, minced
  - 1 can (15 oz) kidney beans, drained
  - 1 can (14 oz) diced tomatoes
  - 2 tablespoons chili powder
  - 1 teaspoon ground cumin
  - Salt and pepper, to taste
- Toppings: shredded lettuce, shredded cheddar cheese, chopped tomatoes, sour cream, sliced jalapeños

A tantalizing blend of Native American and Mexican influences, the Indian Taco stands out. A hearty fry bread serves as the base, topped with chili, lettuce, cheese, and other fixings. Originating in Oklahoma's Indigenous communities, it has become a cherished fusion of flavors that celebrates tradition and innovation in each delectable bite.

Directions

For Fry Bread:
1. In a bowl, mix flour, baking powder, and salt.
2. Gradually add warm water and knead until a dough forms.
3. Divide into balls and flatten into discs.
4. Heat oil in a deep pan. Fry dough until golden and puffed.
5. Drain on paper towels.

For Chili Topping:
1. In a skillet, brown ground meat with chopped onion and garlic.
2. Add beans, diced tomatoes, chili powder, cumin, salt, and pepper. Simmer.

To Assemble:
1. Place fry bread on a plate.
2. Top with chili and desired toppings.
3. Indulge in this unique blend of flavors and cultures!

2 tablespoons

100/serving

5 minutes

Vermont Maple Syrup

Ingredients:

- 100% pure maple syrup, from Vermont's sugar maple trees

Straight from Vermont's maple trees, this liquid gold is a testament to nature's sweetness. The sap of sugar maple trees is transformed into a rich, amber elixir that elevates pancakes, waffles, and more. Drizzle it on, and with each bite, let the essence of Vermont's serene forests and time-honored tradition fill your senses.

Substitutions

- Experiment with different grades of maple syrup for varying flavor profiles.
- Add a touch of cinnamon or vanilla extract to the warmed syrup for extra depth.
- Use maple syrup as a natural sweetener in various recipes, from dressings to desserts.
- Pair with crispy bacon or sausages for a balance of flavors.

Directions

1. Heat the maple syrup in a small saucepan over low heat.
2. Warm it gently until it's ready to be drizzled.
3. Serve it generously over your favorite breakfast delights.
4. Close your eyes and let the sweet embrace of Vermont's maple trees transport you to the heart of the forest.
5. Savor the simplicity and authenticity of this liquid gold.
6. Store any leftovers in a cool, dark place to enjoy nature's sweetness anytime.

1 slice | 320/serving | 75 minutes

Maine Blueberry Pie

Maine's wild blueberries shine in this pie. Their intense flavor is captured in each juicy bite, nestled in a flaky crust. As you savor this pie, imagine the coastal breeze and fields of blue stretching as far as the eye can see. It's a sweet reminder of Maine's enchanting landscapes and the magic that happens when summer meets dessert.

Ingredients:

- For Crust:
  - 2 1/2 cups all-purpose flour
  - 1 teaspoon salt
  - 1 cup unsalted butter, cold and cubed
  - 6-8 tablespoons ice water
- For Filling:
  - 5 cups fresh blueberries
  - 3/4 cup granulated sugar
  - 1/4 cup cornstarch
  - 1 tablespoon lemon juice
  - Zest of 1 lemon
  - 1/2 teaspoon cinnamon
  - Egg wash (1 egg beaten with 1 tablespoon water)
  - Coarse sugar, for sprinkling

Directions

For Crust:
1. In a food processor, pulse flour and salt.
2. Add cold butter and pulse until pea-sized crumbs form.
3. Gradually add ice water and pulse until dough comes together.
4. Divide into two discs, wrap, and chill.

For Filling:
1. In a bowl, combine blueberries, sugar, cornstarch, lemon juice, zest, and cinnamon.
2. Roll out one pie crust and place in a pie dish.
3. Fill with blueberry mixture.
4. Roll out the second crust and lay over the filling. Trim and seal edges.
5. Brush with egg wash and sprinkle with coarse sugar.
6. Bake at 375°F (190°C) for about 50-60 minutes, until golden and bubbly.
7. Let cool before diving into a slice of Maine's blueberry bounty!

1 bowl

280/se rving

60 minutes

New England Clam Chowder

Ingredients:

- 2 dozen fresh clams, scrubbed and cleaned
- 3 slices bacon, chopped
- 1 onion, finely chopped
- 2 potatoes, diced
- 2 cups half-and-half cream
- 1 cup chicken or vegetable broth
- 2 tablespoons butter
- 2 tablespoons all-purpose flour
- Salt and pepper, to taste
- Fresh chives, chopped, for garnish

Substitutions

- Swap fresh clams with canned clams if fresh aren't available.
- Use cubed ham instead of bacon for a different flavor dimension.
- Incorporate thyme or dill for a herbal touch.
- Serve in sourdough bread bowls for an indulgent presentation.

The crown jewel of chowders! This creamy delight hails from the heart of Massachusetts and captures the essence of the New England coastline. Imagine tender clams, diced potatoes, and aromatic vegetables luxuriating in a velvety, white broth. A spoonful is like a warm hug from the sea, inviting you to indulge in the comforts of the coast.

Directions

1. In a pot, cook bacon over medium heat until crispy. Remove and set aside.
2. Sauté chopped onion until translucent.
3. Add diced potatoes and just enough water to cover them. Simmer until potatoes are tender.
4. In another pot, melt butter and whisk in flour to create a roux.
5. Gradually whisk in half-and-half and broth. Cook until thickened.
6. Add cooked bacon, clams (with juices), and cooked potatoes.
7. Simmer until flavors meld. Season with salt and pepper.
8. Ladle into bowls, garnish with chopped chives.
9. Immerse yourself in the creamy embrace of New England's coastal flavors.

1 bowl

220/se
rving

60
minutes

Maryland Crab Soup

Ingredients:

- 1 lb lump crab meat
- 1 onion, chopped
- 2 carrots, diced
- 2 celery stalks, diced
- 2 potatoes, diced
- 1 can (14 oz) diced tomatoes
- 4 cups chicken or vegetable broth
- 1 teaspoon Old Bay seasoning
- 1/2 teaspoon paprika
- Hot sauce, to taste
- Salt and pepper, to taste
- Chopped fresh parsley, for garnish

Substitutions

- Use lump crab meat for the best texture and flavor.
- Customize the spice level with more or less hot sauce.
- Add a dash of Worcestershire sauce for a savory kick.
- Serve with oyster crackers or crusty bread for a satisfying meal.

A taste of the Chesapeake Bay! Maryland Crab Soup is a celebration of the sea's bounty, with succulent crab meat as the star. This tomato-based soup is enriched with vegetables and spices, creating a medley of flavors that pay homage to the East Coast's maritime heritage. Dip your spoon and embark on a culinary journey along Maryland's coastal charm.

Directions

1. In a pot, sauté chopped onion until translucent.
2. Add diced carrots, celery, and potatoes. Sauté briefly.
3. Pour in diced tomatoes and broth. Bring to a simmer.
4. Season with Old Bay seasoning, paprika, hot sauce, salt, and pepper.
5. Simmer until vegetables are tender.
6. Gently fold in lump crab meat.
7. Let the soup warm through.
8. Ladle into bowls, garnish with chopped parsley.
9. Enjoy the taste of Maryland's coastal traditions with every spoonful!

Chapter 2:
Southern Comfort

2 pieces · **300/serving** · **45 minutes**

Southern Fried Chicken

Ingredients:

- 4 chicken pieces (legs, thighs, wings, or breasts)
- 2 cups buttermilk
- 2 cups all-purpose flour
- 1 tablespoon paprika
- 1 tablespoon garlic powder
- 1 tablespoon onion powder
- 1 teaspoon cayenne pepper
- Salt and pepper, to taste
- Vegetable oil, for frying

Substitutions

- For a spicier kick, add more cayenne pepper to the flour mixture.
- Use boneless chicken pieces for a quicker cooking time.
- Swap buttermilk with whole milk for a lighter marinade.
- Experiment with different herbs and spices for your own unique blend of flavors.

A true Southern classic: crispy, golden-fried chicken. This dish is more than just food; it's a tradition that brings families and communities together. The crispy coating encases tender, juicy meat that's been marinated and seasoned to perfection. Let each bite transport you to a Southern porch, where the flavors and warmth embrace you like an old friend.

Directions

1. Place chicken pieces in a bowl and cover with buttermilk. Marinate for at least 1 hour or overnight.
2. In a shallow dish, mix flour, paprika, garlic powder, onion powder, cayenne pepper, salt, and pepper.
3. Remove chicken from buttermilk and let excess drip off.
4. Dredge chicken in the seasoned flour mixture, pressing gently to adhere.
5. Heat oil in a deep skillet to 350°F (175°C).
6. Fry chicken until golden and cooked through, about 15-20 minutes.
7. Drain on paper towels.
8. Serve hot and crispy, and relish in the heartwarming taste of Southern hospitality.

1
serving

380/se
rving

30
minutes

Grits and Shrimp

Ingredients:

- 1 cup stone-ground grits
- 4 cups chicken or vegetable broth
- 1 cup grated cheddar cheese
- 1/4 cup butter
- 1 lb large shrimp, peeled and deveined
- 1 tablespoon Cajun seasoning
- 1 tablespoon paprika
- 1 tablespoon olive oil
- 2 cloves garlic, minced
- Salt and pepper, to taste
- Chopped fresh parsley, for garnish

Substitutions

- Replace cheddar cheese with other varieties for a different flavor profile.
- Customize the level of spiciness with more or less Cajun seasoning.
- Add diced bell peppers and onions to the shrimp for extra texture and flavor.
- Drizzle with a squeeze of fresh lemon juice for a burst of acidity.

A dish that's both humble and indulgent, Grits and Shrimp showcases Southern comfort at its best. Creamy, buttery grits serve as the backdrop for succulent shrimp sautéed with spices and aromatics. With each spoonful, savor the contrast between the smooth grits and the bold flavors of the shrimp. It's a taste of the South that warms the heart and satisfies the soul.

Directions

1. In a pot, bring chicken or vegetable broth to a boil.
2. Gradually whisk in grits and reduce heat to low. Cook, stirring occasionally, until creamy and tender.
3. Stir in grated cheddar cheese and butter until melted.
4. In a skillet, heat olive oil over medium heat.
5. Sauté minced garlic until fragrant, then add shrimp.
6. Sprinkle Cajun seasoning, paprika, salt, and pepper over the shrimp. Cook until pink and opaque.
7. Serve shrimp over a bed of creamy grits.
8. Garnish with chopped parsley and let the Southern flavors take you on a culinary journey.

1
serving

350/se
rving

120
minutes

Cajun Crawfish Boil

Ingredients:

- 5 lbs live crawfish, purged and cleaned
- 6 ears corn, shucked and halved
- 2 lbs small red potatoes
- 1 lb smoked sausage or Andouille sausage, cut into chunks
- 4 lemons, halved
- 1 onion, quartered
- 1 head garlic, halved
- 2 tablespoons Cajun seasoning
- 1 tablespoon Old Bay seasoning
- 1 tablespoon cayenne pepper
- Salt, to taste
- Hot sauce, for serving
- Fresh parsley, for garnish

Substitutions

- Swap crawfish with shrimp if crawfish aren't available in your area.
- Include whole garlic cloves and halved artichokes for added variety.
- Adjust the spice level by increasing or decreasing the cayenne pepper.
- Offer melted butter or garlic aioli for dipping.

A lively feast straight from the bayous of Louisiana, the Cajun Crawfish Boil is a communal gathering of friends and family. Crawfish, corn, potatoes, and sausages are boiled with a robust blend of Cajun spices. It's not just a meal—it's an event that celebrates the rich culture and zest for life found in every corner of the South. Get ready to roll up your sleeves and dive in!

Directions

1. Fill a large pot with water and bring to a boil.
2. Add Cajun seasoning, Old Bay seasoning, cayenne pepper, salt, lemons, onion, and garlic.
3. Once the water is seasoned and aromatic, add potatoes. Cook for 15-20 minutes.
4. Add sausage and corn. Cook for an additional 10 minutes.
5. Add crawfish and cook for 2-3 minutes until they turn bright red.
6. Drain and dump the contents onto a table covered with newspaper or butcher paper.
7. Sprinkle with chopped parsley.
8. Serve with hot sauce and let the Cajun festivities begin!

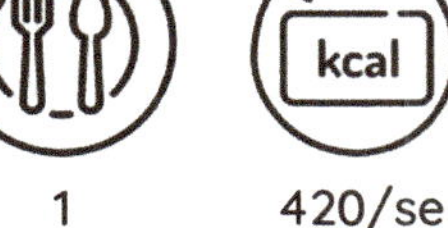

1
serving

420/se
rving

30
minutes

Biscuits and Gravy

Ingredients:

- For Biscuits:
  - 2 cups all-purpose flour
  - 1 tablespoon baking powder
  - 1/2 teaspoon salt
  - 1/2 cup unsalted butter, cold and cubed
  - 3/4 cup buttermilk
- For Gravy:
  - 1/2 lb breakfast sausage
  - 1/4 cup all-purpose flour
  - 2 cups milk
  - Salt and pepper, to taste
- Fresh chopped parsley, for garnish

Substitutions

- Swap buttermilk biscuits with store-bought ones for a quicker version.
- Use ground turkey or plant-based sausage for a lighter gravy.
- Add a dash of nutmeg or sage to the gravy for extra flavor.
- Serve with a fried egg on top for a hearty breakfast twist.

Directions

For Biscuits:
1. Preheat oven to 425°F (220°C). Line a baking sheet with parchment paper.
2. In a bowl, whisk flour, baking powder, and salt.
3. Cut in cold butter until mixture resembles coarse crumbs.
4. Stir in buttermilk until just combined. Turn out onto a floured surface.
5. Pat dough into a rectangle and fold in thirds like a letter.
6. Repeat the folding process 2-3 times.
7. Roll out dough and cut biscuits. Place on baking sheet and bake for 15-20 minutes.

For Gravy:
1. Cook sausage in a skillet over medium heat, breaking it into crumbles. Remove sausage and set aside.
2. In the same skillet, leave about 2 tablespoons of sausage drippings. Add flour and cook, stirring, for 2 minutes to make a roux.
3. Gradually whisk in milk and cook until thickened.
4. Return cooked sausage to the gravy. Season with salt and pepper.
5. Split biscuits in half and spoon gravy over each half.
6. Garnish with chopped parsley and dive into this Southern comfort classic!

1
serving

400/se
rving

40
minutes

Shrimp and Grits

Ingredients:

- 1/2 cup stone-ground grits
- 2 cups chicken or vegetable broth
- 1/2 cup grated cheddar cheese
- 1/4 cup heavy cream
- 1/4 cup butter
- 1/2 lb large shrimp, peeled and deveined
- 4 slices bacon, chopped
- 1/2 onion, finely chopped
- 1/2 bell pepper, finely chopped
- 1 clove garlic, minced
- 1/4 teaspoon Old Bay seasoning
- Salt and pepper, to taste
- Chopped fresh chives, for garnish

Substitutions

- Use quick-cooking grits for a faster preparation.
- Replace cheddar cheese with smoked Gouda for a more robust flavor.
- Add a splash of white wine to the shrimp for an extra layer of depth.
- Incorporate chopped tomatoes for a burst of freshness.

Another ode to the South, Shrimp and Grits embodies comfort with a touch of elegance. Creamy, cheesy grits serve as the base for tender shrimp sautéed with smoky bacon, aromatic vegetables, and a hint of spice. With each spoonful, enjoy the harmony of flavors and textures—a dish that's equally at home on a farmhouse table or a fine dining setting.

Directions

1. In a pot, bring chicken or vegetable broth to a boil.
2. Gradually whisk in grits and reduce heat to low. Cook, stirring occasionally, until creamy and tender.
3. Stir in grated cheddar cheese, heavy cream, and butter until melted.
4. In a skillet, cook chopped bacon until crispy. Remove bacon and set aside.
5. In the same skillet, sauté chopped onion, bell pepper, and minced garlic until softened.
6. Add shrimp and Old Bay seasoning. Cook until shrimp are pink and opaque.
7. Stir in cooked bacon and season with salt and pepper.
8. Serve shrimp over a bed of creamy grits.
9. Garnish with chopped chives and savor the harmonious blend of flavors.

1 piece

380/se rving

45 minutes

Texas Sheet Cake

Ingredients:

- For Cake:
  - 2 cups all-purpose flour
  - 2 cups granulated sugar
  - 1 teaspoon baking soda
  - 1/2 teaspoon salt
  - 1 cup unsalted butter
  - 1 cup water
  - 1/4 cup cocoa powder
  - 1/2 cup buttermilk
  - 2 large eggs
  - 1 teaspoon vanilla extract
- For Icing:
  - 1/2 cup unsalted butter
  - 1/4 cup cocoa powder
  - 1/3 cup milk
  - 4 cups powdered sugar
  - 1 teaspoon vanilla extract
  - 1 cup chopped pecans
- Additional chopped pecans, for garnish

Directions

For Cake:
1. Preheat oven to 350°F (175°C). Grease a large baking sheet.
2. In a bowl, whisk flour, sugar, baking soda, and salt.
3. In a saucepan, combine butter, water, and cocoa powder. Bring to a boil, then pour over the dry ingredients.
4. Mix in buttermilk, eggs, and vanilla until well combined.
5. Pour batter onto the prepared baking sheet and spread evenly.
6. Bake for 20-25 minutes until a toothpick comes out clean.

For Icing:
1. In a saucepan, melt butter. Stir in cocoa powder and milk.
2. Bring to a boil, then remove from heat.
3. Whisk in powdered sugar and vanilla until smooth.
4. Stir in chopped pecans.
5. Pour icing over the warm cake and spread evenly.
6. Garnish with additional chopped pecans.
7. Let the cake cool and the icing set before cutting into squares and enjoying a piece of Texas-sized sweetness.

1
serving

320/se
rving

60
minutes

Peach Cobbler

A dessert that embodies the essence of summer, Peach Cobbler is a true Southern delight. Juicy, ripe peaches are baked beneath a layer of buttery, spiced biscuit dough. The result is a comforting dessert that captures the flavors of the orchard and the warmth of Southern hospitality. Served warm with a scoop of vanilla ice cream, each bite is a taste of sunshine and sweetness.

Ingredients:

- 4 cups fresh or canned sliced peaches, drained
- 1 cup granulated sugar
- 1/4 teaspoon ground cinnamon
- 1/2 cup unsalted butter
- 1 cup all-purpose flour
- 1 cup granulated sugar
- 1 tablespoon baking powder
- 1/2 teaspoon salt
- 1 cup milk
- 1 teaspoon vanilla extract
- Ground nutmeg, for sprinkling
- Vanilla ice cream, for serving

Directions

1. Preheat oven to 375°F (190°C). Place butter in a baking dish and melt in the preheating oven.
2. In a saucepan, combine peaches, sugar, and ground cinnamon. Cook over medium heat until sugar is dissolved and peaches are softened.
3. In a bowl, whisk flour, sugar, baking powder, and salt.
4. Stir in milk and vanilla until a smooth batter forms.
5. Pour batter over melted butter in the baking dish.
6. Spoon peaches over the batter, distributing them evenly.
7. Sprinkle ground nutmeg over the top.
8. Bake for 40-45 minutes until golden and bubbly.
9. Serve warm with a scoop of vanilla ice cream.
10. Relish in the heartwarming flavors of Southern summer in every spoonful.

Substitutions

- Replace peaches with other fruits like berries, apples, or cherries for variety.
- Use brown sugar instead of granulated sugar for a deeper flavor.
- Add a pinch of ground cloves to the peaches for a hint of warmth.
- Drizzle with caramel sauce for an extra layer of indulgence.

2
tablesp
oons

50/ser
ving

10
minutes

Alabama White BBQ Sauce

Ingredients:

- 1 cup mayonnaise
- 1/4 cup apple cider vinegar
- 2 tablespoons prepared horseradish
- 1 teaspoon Dijon mustard
- 1 teaspoon granulated sugar
- 1/2 teaspoon salt
- 1/2 teaspoon black pepper
- 1/4 teaspoon garlic powder
- 1/4 teaspoon onion powder
- 1/4 teaspoon cayenne pepper
- 1/4 teaspoon smoked paprika
- Lemon juice, to taste
- Fresh chopped parsley, for garnish

Substitutions

- Experiment with different types of vinegar, like white wine vinegar or rice vinegar.
- Adjust the horseradish and cayenne pepper to your preferred level of spiciness.
- Add a splash of hot sauce for an extra kick.
- Use Greek yogurt or sour cream as a mayo alternative for a tangy twist.

A unique and tangy creation, Alabama White BBQ Sauce stands out in a sea of red. This mayo-based sauce is infused with vinegar, horseradish, and spices, creating a zesty complement to grilled meats. Popular in Alabama, it's a testament to the South's creative culinary spirit. Try it as a marinade, dip, or drizzle and experience the harmonious balance of flavors.

Directions

1. In a bowl, whisk together mayonnaise, apple cider vinegar, horseradish, and Dijon mustard.
2. Add granulated sugar, salt, black pepper, garlic powder, onion powder, cayenne pepper, and smoked paprika. Mix well.
3. Add a squeeze of lemon juice to brighten the flavors and balance the tanginess.
4. Adjust seasoning to taste, adding more lemon juice if desired.
5. Let the flavors meld in the refrigerator for at least 30 minutes before serving.
6. Drizzle, dip, or slather this white BBQ sauce on your favorite grilled dishes.
7. Garnish with chopped parsley for a fresh finish.
8. Celebrate the creativity of Southern BBQ traditions with this zesty creation!

1 slice

420/se
rving

60
minutes

Mississippi Mud Pie

Ingredients:

- For Crust:
  - 1 1/2 cups chocolate cookie crumbs
  - 6 tablespoons unsalted butter, melted
- For Filling:
  - 1 1/4 cups semisweet chocolate chips
  - 1/2 cup unsalted butter
  - 3/4 cup granulated sugar
  - 1 teaspoon vanilla extract
  - 3 large eggs
- For Topping:
  - 1 cup heavy cream
  - 2 tablespoons powdered sugar
  - Chocolate shavings, for garnish

Substitutions

- Swap chocolate cookie crumbs for graham cracker crumbs or Oreo crumbs.
- Add a splash of coffee or espresso to the chocolate filling for a deeper flavor.
- Use chocolate curls or grated chocolate for the topping.
- Serve with a scoop of coffee or vanilla ice cream for a delightful contrast.

Directions

For Crust:
1. Preheat oven to 350°F (175°C). Mix chocolate cookie crumbs and melted butter.
2. Press mixture into a pie dish to form the crust. Bake for 10 minutes.
3. Let the crust cool while preparing the filling.

For Filling:
1. Melt chocolate chips and butter in a double boiler, stirring until smooth.
2. Remove from heat and stir in granulated sugar and vanilla extract.
3. Beat in eggs, one at a time, until well incorporated.
4. Pour filling into the cooled crust and smooth the top.
5. Chill in the refrigerator until set, about 2-3 hours.

For Topping:
1. Whip heavy cream and powdered sugar until stiff peaks form.
2. Spread whipped cream over the pie filling.
3. Garnish with chocolate shavings for an elegant touch.
4. Slice and indulge in the velvety richness of Mississippi Mud Pie.

6 pieces

180/ser
ving

30
minutes

Hushpuppies

Ingredients:

- 1 cup cornmeal
- 1/2 cup all-purpose flour
- 1 teaspoon baking powder
- 1/2 teaspoon salt
- 1/2 teaspoon onion powder
- 1/4 teaspoon garlic powder
- 1/4 teaspoon paprika
- 1/4 teaspoon black pepper
- 1/2 cup buttermilk
- 1/4 cup grated onion
- 1 large egg
- Vegetable oil, for frying

Substitutions

- Add chopped jalapeños or cheese to the batter for extra flavor and heat.
- Replace grated onion with chopped scallions for a different twist.
- Dip hushpuppies in honey or a savory dipping sauce for a delightful contrast.
- Try using a mix of cornmeal and corn flour for a lighter texture.

These golden nuggets of goodness are a Southern side dish staple. Hushpuppies are a delicious blend of cornmeal, buttermilk, and spices, deep-fried to perfection. Whether served as a snack, appetizer, or side, they're a crunchy and flavorful addition to any meal. The name "hushpuppies" has its own charming history—it's said to come from using these treats to "hush" barking dogs!

Directions

1. In a bowl, whisk together cornmeal, flour, baking powder, salt, onion powder, garlic powder, paprika, and black pepper.
2. In another bowl, mix buttermilk, grated onion, and egg until well combined.
3. Combine wet and dry ingredients and stir until just incorporated.
4. Heat vegetable oil in a deep skillet to 350°F (175°C).
5. Using a spoon, drop scoops of batter into the hot oil.
6. Fry until golden brown, turning occasionally to cook evenly.
7. Remove hushpuppies and drain on paper towels.
8. Serve warm and crispy, embracing the Southern tradition of hushing your hunger!

Chapter 3:
Midwest Flavors

1 slice

400/se rving

120 minutes

Chicago Deep Dish Pizza

Ingredients:

- For Crust:
  - 3 cups all-purpose flour
  - 1/4 cup yellow cornmeal
  - 1 teaspoon salt
  - 1 tablespoon granulated sugar
  - 1 packet active dry yeast
  - 1 1/4 cups warm water
  - 1/4 cup olive oil
- For Filling:
  - 2 cups shredded mozzarella cheese
  - 1/2 lb Italian sausage, cooked and crumbled
  - 1 cup chunky tomato sauce
  - 1 teaspoon dried oregano
  - 1/2 teaspoon garlic powder
  - Salt and pepper, to taste
  - Grated Parmesan cheese, for sprinkling
- Olive oil, for drizzling

Directions

For Crust:
1. In a bowl, whisk flour, cornmeal, salt, and sugar.
2. In another bowl, dissolve yeast in warm water and let stand for 5 minutes.
3. Mix yeast mixture and olive oil into dry ingredients until a dough forms.
4. Knead dough on a floured surface until smooth.
5. Grease a deep-dish pizza pan and press dough into the pan, covering the bottom and sides.
6. Let dough rise for about 30 minutes.

For Filling:
1. Preheat oven to 425°F (220°C).
2. Layer shredded mozzarella, cooked sausage, and chunky tomato sauce in the crust.
3. Sprinkle with oregano, garlic powder, salt, and pepper.
4. Drizzle with olive oil and sprinkle with grated Parmesan cheese.
5. Bake for 25-30 minutes, until golden and bubbly.
6. Let the pizza cool slightly before slicing and experiencing the Chicago magic.

1
serving

350/se
rving

90
minutes

Cincinnati Chili

Ingredients:

- 1 lb ground beef
- 1 onion, chopped
- 2 cloves garlic, minced
- 2 cups beef broth
- 1 can (15 oz) tomato sauce
- 2 tablespoons chili powder
- 1 teaspoon ground cinnamon
- 1/2 teaspoon ground allspice
- 1/2 teaspoon ground cloves
- 1 tablespoon unsweetened cocoa powder
- Salt and pepper, to taste
- Cooked spaghetti, for serving
- Shredded cheddar cheese, chopped onions, kidney beans, and oyster crackers, for topping

A taste of Ohio's comfort, Cincinnati Chili is a unique dish that's as versatile as it is delicious. Ground beef is simmered with spices like cinnamon, cloves, and cocoa powder, resulting in a complex and savory flavor profile. Serve it over spaghetti or as a topping for hot dogs, and don't forget the traditional toppings like shredded cheese and chopped onions.

Directions

1. In a pot, cook ground beef over medium heat until browned. Drain excess fat.
2. Add chopped onion and minced garlic. Cook until onion is softened.
3. Stir in beef broth and tomato sauce. Bring to a simmer.
4. Add chili powder, ground cinnamon, allspice, ground cloves, cocoa powder, salt, and pepper.
5. Simmer for about 1 hour, allowing the flavors to meld.
6. Serve Cincinnati chili over cooked spaghetti.
7. Top with shredded cheddar cheese, chopped onions, kidney beans, and oyster crackers.
8. Savor the unique harmony of spices in this Midwest favorite.

1
serving

280/se
rving

20
minutes

Cheese Curds

Ingredients:

- 1 lb fresh cheese curds
- 1 cup all-purpose flour
- 1 teaspoon baking powder
- 1/2 teaspoon salt
- 1 cup cold water
- Vegetable oil, for frying

Substitutions

- Use different types of cheese curds, like cheddar, mozzarella, or pepper jack, for variety.
- Add a pinch of cayenne pepper or paprika to the batter for a touch of heat.
- Substitute sparkling water for a lighter, crispier batter.
- Serve with a side of marinara sauce or garlic aioli for dipping.

A Wisconsin classic, Cheese Curds are a celebration of dairy at its finest. These bite-sized morsels are made from fresh cheese curds that are coated in a light batter and deep-fried until golden and crispy. Squeaky and addictive, they're a must-try Midwest treat that captures the essence of cheese country. Dip them in your favorite sauce and enjoy the cheesy delight.

Directions

1. In a bowl, whisk together flour, baking powder, and salt.
2. Gradually add cold water and mix until a smooth batter forms.
3. Heat vegetable oil in a deep skillet to 375°F (190°C).
4. Dip cheese curds into the batter, letting excess batter drip off.
5. Carefully place coated curds into the hot oil.
6. Fry for about 2-3 minutes until golden and crispy.
7. Remove with a slotted spoon and drain on paper towels.
8. Serve the cheese curds while they're still warm and squeaky!
9. Dip in ketchup, ranch dressing, or your favorite sauce.
10. Experience the delightful combination of gooey cheese and crunchy batter.

1
serving

300/se
rving

60
minutes

Minnesota Hot Dish

Ingredients:

- 1 lb ground beef
- 1 onion, chopped
- 1 can (10.5 oz) condensed cream of mushroom soup
- 1 can (10.5 oz) condensed cream of chicken soup
- 1 cup frozen mixed vegetables
- 1 cup shredded cheddar cheese
- 1 cup milk
- Salt and pepper, to taste
- 4 cups frozen tater tots

Substitutions

- Customize the vegetables to your liking, using options like peas, carrots, or corn.
- Replace ground beef with ground turkey or a meatless alternative for a lighter version.
- Add a sprinkle of dried thyme or rosemary for extra flavor.
- Serve with a dollop of sour cream or a drizzle of hot sauce for a tangy kick.

A casserole that's synonymous with Midwest comfort, Minnesota Hot Dish is a medley of ground beef, vegetables, and creamy goodness. Topped with tater tots and baked until golden, this dish is a nostalgic taste of home. It's a staple at potlucks, family gatherings, and cozy dinners—bringing together flavors that warm the heart and create lasting memories.

Directions

1. Preheat oven to 350°F (175°C). Grease a baking dish.
2. In a skillet, cook ground beef and chopped onion until beef is browned. Drain excess fat.
3. In a bowl, mix together cream of mushroom soup, cream of chicken soup, mixed vegetables, shredded cheddar cheese, and milk.
4. Stir in cooked ground beef and onion. Season with salt and pepper.
5. Pour mixture into the greased baking dish.
6. Arrange frozen tater tots on top of the mixture in an even layer.
7. Bake for 30-35 minutes until tater tots are golden and the casserole is bubbly.
8. Let the hot dish cool slightly before digging in and enjoying a taste of Midwest comfort.

1 sandwich

450/serving

30 minutes

Iowa Pork Tenderloin Sandwich

Ingredients:

- 1 lb pork tenderloin, trimmed and pounded thin
- 1 cup all-purpose flour
- 2 large eggs, beaten
- 2 cups breadcrumbs (preferably panko)
- 1 teaspoon paprika
- Salt and pepper, to taste
- Vegetable oil, for frying
- Hamburger buns
- Lettuce, tomato slices, onion slices, and pickles, for topping

Substitutions

- Add a touch of cayenne pepper to the breadcrumbs for a hint of heat.
- Swap pork tenderloin with chicken breast or a breaded Portobello mushroom for a different twist.
- Create a signature sauce using mayo, mustard, and a dash of hot sauce.
- Serve with a side of coleslaw or potato chips for a complete meal.

A beloved Iowa classic, the Pork Tenderloin Sandwich is a culinary masterpiece that's as big as the heartland. A tender and juicy pork tenderloin is pounded thin, breaded, and fried to golden perfection. Served on a bun and topped with traditional fixings, this sandwich is a testament to Midwest pride and hearty appetites. Get ready for a sandwich that's larger than life!

Directions

1. Preheat oil in a deep skillet to 350°F (175°C).
2. In separate bowls, place flour, beaten eggs, and breadcrumbs.
3. Season breadcrumbs with paprika, salt, and pepper.
4. Dredge pork tenderloin in flour, shaking off excess.
5. Dip in beaten eggs, letting excess drip off.
6. Coat with seasoned breadcrumbs, pressing gently to adhere.
7. Carefully place breaded pork in hot oil and fry until golden and cooked through, about 3-4 minutes per side.
8. Drain on paper towels.
9. Toast hamburger buns and assemble sandwiches with lettuce, tomato slices, onion slices, pickles, and a generous slice of fried pork tenderloin.
10. Enjoy the hearty flavors of Iowa's pride between two buns!

1 pasty   420/serving   90 minutes

Pasties

Ingredients:

- For Dough:
  - 2 1/2 cups all-purpose flour
  - 1/2 teaspoon salt
  - 1 cup unsalted butter, cold and cubed
  - 1/2 cup ice water
- For Filling:
  - 1 lb ground beef
  - 1 onion, chopped
  - 2 cups diced potatoes
  - 1 cup diced rutabaga
  - 1 cup diced carrot
  - Salt and pepper, to taste
  - 2 tablespoons butter
  - 1 egg, beaten
- Ketchup or gravy, for serving

Substitutions

- Replace ground beef with ground pork or a mix of ground meats for variation.
- Swap rutabaga with turnips or additional potatoes.
- Customize the filling with peas, corn, or other favorite vegetables.
- Try a sprinkle of thyme or rosemary for extra herbal flavor.
- Serve with a side of coleslaw or a green salad for a balanced meal.

Directions

For Dough:
1. In a bowl, whisk flour and salt.
2. Cut in cold butter until mixture resembles coarse crumbs.
3. Gradually add ice water and mix until dough comes together.
4. Shape dough into a disc, wrap in plastic, and refrigerate for at least 30 minutes.

For Filling:
1. In a skillet, cook ground beef and chopped onion until beef is browned. Drain excess fat.
2. In a bowl, combine cooked beef, diced potatoes, diced rutabaga, and diced carrot.
3. Season with salt and pepper.
4. Roll out chilled dough and cut into circles.
5. Place filling on one half of each dough circle.
6. Dot filling with butter and fold dough over to encase the filling.
7. Crimp edges to seal the pasties.
8. Brush pasties with beaten egg for a golden crust.
9. Bake at 375°F (190°C) for about 45-50 minutes until pasties are golden and the filling is cooked.
10. Serve with ketchup or gravy and experience the comfort of a classic Upper Peninsula meal.

1
serving

350/se
rving

30
minutes

Sloppy Joe

Ingredients:

- 1 lb ground beef
- 1/2 onion, chopped
- 1/2 bell pepper, chopped
- 2 cloves garlic, minced
- 1 can (15 oz) tomato sauce
- 2 tablespoons tomato paste
- 2 tablespoons brown sugar
- 1 tablespoon Worcestershire sauce
- 1 teaspoon yellow mustard
- 1/2 teaspoon chili powder
- Salt and pepper, to taste
- Hamburger buns

Substitutions

- Add a touch of cayenne pepper or hot sauce for extra heat.
- Incorporate diced jalapeños or green chilies for a spicy twist.
- Swap ground beef with ground turkey or plant-based meat for a lighter version.
- Top with shredded cheese or a dollop of sour cream for extra creaminess.
- Serve with pickles or pickled jalapeños for a tangy kick.

A timeless classic that's messy and marvelous, Sloppy Joe is a beloved Midwest creation. Ground beef is simmered in a tangy tomato-based sauce, creating a flavorful filling that's as satisfying as it is saucy. Served on a soft bun, this sandwich is a taste of childhood nostalgia and a reminder that comfort food never goes out of style.

Directions

1. In a skillet, cook ground beef, chopped onion, chopped bell pepper, and minced garlic until beef is browned.
2. Drain excess fat.
3. Stir in tomato sauce and tomato paste.
4. Add brown sugar, Worcestershire sauce, yellow mustard, chili powder, salt, and pepper.
5. Simmer for about 10-15 minutes, allowing flavors to meld.
6. Toast hamburger buns.
7. Spoon the Sloppy Joe filling onto the buns.
8. Serve with a side of coleslaw or potato chips for a classic pairing.
9. Embrace the joy of indulging in a messy, flavorful Sloppy Joe sandwich.

1
bratwur
st

350/se
rving

30
minutes

Wisconsin Bratwurst

Ingredients:

- 4 bratwurst sausages
- 4 bratwurst buns
- 1 onion, thinly sliced
- 1 cup sauerkraut, drained and rinsed
- Mustard, for serving

Substitutions

- Use different types of sausages, like cheddar bratwurst or beer bratwurst, for variety.
- Grill the buns for a toasted and slightly smoky flavor.
- Serve with a side of German potato salad or coleslaw for a complete meal.
- Add a sprinkle of chopped fresh herbs, like parsley or chives, for extra freshness.
- Include diced tomatoes, pickles, or relish for additional toppings.

A Wisconsin pride, the Bratwurst is a flavorful sausage that's a staple at cookouts, tailgates, and festivals. Made with a blend of pork and spices, these sausages are grilled to perfection and nestled in a soft bun. Top with sautéed onions, sauerkraut, and mustard, and you've got a taste of Wisconsin's culinary heritage. Grab a brat and join the flavor party!

Directions

1. Preheat grill to medium-high heat.
2. Grill bratwurst sausages, turning occasionally, until cooked through and nicely browned, about 15-20 minutes.
3. While sausages are grilling, sauté thinly sliced onions in a skillet until golden and caramelized.
4. Warm sauerkraut in a separate skillet or in the microwave.
5. Toast bratwurst buns on the grill for a minute or two until slightly crispy.
6. Place grilled bratwurst sausages in buns.
7. Top with sautéed onions and sauerkraut.
8. Squeeze mustard over the sausages and enjoy the mouthwatering flavors of Wisconsin.

1 runza   400/serving   120 minutes

Nebraska Runza

Ingredients:

- For Dough:
  - 4 cups all-purpose flour
  - 1 packet active dry yeast
  - 1/4 cup granulated sugar
  - 1/2 teaspoon salt
  - 3/4 cup milk
  - 1/2 cup water
  - 1/4 cup unsalted butter
- For Filling:
  - 1 lb ground beef
  - 1 onion, chopped
  - 4 cups finely chopped cabbage
  - Salt and pepper, to taste
- Egg wash (1 beaten egg mixed with 1 tablespoon water)
- Caraway seeds, for topping

Directions

For Dough:
1. In a bowl, whisk together flour, yeast, sugar, and salt.
2. In a saucepan, heat milk, water, and butter until warm.
3. Add wet ingredients to dry ingredients and mix until a dough forms.
4. Knead dough on a floured surface until smooth and elastic.
5. Place dough in a greased bowl, cover, and let rise until doubled in size, about 1 hour.

For Filling:
1. In a skillet, cook ground beef and chopped onion until beef is browned. Drain excess fat.
2. Add finely chopped cabbage and cook until wilted and tender.
3. Season with salt and pepper.
4. Punch down risen dough and divide into portions.
5. Roll each portion into an oval shape.
6. Spoon filling onto one half of each oval dough piece.
7. Fold dough over the filling and pinch edges to seal.
8. Place runzas on a baking sheet, seam side down.
9. Brush with egg wash and sprinkle with caraway seeds.
10. Bake at 350°F (175°C) for about 20-25 minutes until runzas are golden and baked through.
11. Enjoy the satisfying flavors of Nebraska in every bite.

1 serving

400/serving

240 minutes

Kansas BBQ Brisket

Ingredients:

- 1 whole beef brisket (10-12 lbs)
- For Dry Rub:
 - 1/4 cup brown sugar
 - 2 tablespoons paprika
 - 1 tablespoon black pepper
 - 1 tablespoon salt
 - 1 tablespoon chili powder
 - 1 tablespoon garlic powder
 - 1 tablespoon onion powder
 - 1 teaspoon cayenne pepper
- For BBQ Sauce (Optional):
 - 1 cup ketchup
 - 1/2 cup apple cider vinegar
 - 1/4 cup brown sugar
 - 2 tablespoons molasses
 - 1 tablespoon Worcestershire sauce
 - 1 teaspoon garlic powder
 - 1/2 teaspoon black pepper
- Wood chips or chunks (hickory or oak), for smoking

Directions

For Dry Rub:
1. In a bowl, combine brown sugar, paprika, black pepper, salt, chili powder, garlic powder, onion powder, and cayenne pepper.
2. Pat the brisket dry with paper towels and generously coat with the dry rub, pressing the rub into the meat.
3. Wrap the brisket in plastic wrap and refrigerate for at least 4 hours or overnight.

For Smoking:
1. Prepare your smoker according to manufacturer's instructions, maintaining a temperature of 225-250°F (107-121°C).
2. Place the brisket in the smoker and add wood chips or chunks for smoke flavor.
3. Smoke the brisket for about 1.5 to 2 hours per pound, or until the internal temperature reaches 195-203°F (90-95°C). This can take anywhere from 8 to 12 hours.
4. Baste the brisket with BBQ sauce during the last hour of smoking, if desired.
5. Once the brisket reaches the desired temperature, remove it from the smoker and let it rest for at least 30 minutes before slicing.
6. Slice against the grain and serve with additional BBQ sauce, if desired.
7. Experience the art of Kansas BBQ with every tender and smoky bite.

Chapter 4: Western Inspirations

1 slice

150/ser
ving

180
minutes

California Sourdough Bread

A slice of the West Coast's charm, California Sourdough Bread is a masterpiece of tangy flavor and chewy texture. Crafted through a process of wild yeast fermentation, this bread has a crisp crust and a soft, airy interior. It's a reflection of California's laid-back vibes and artisanal spirit—perfect for smearing with butter or creating the ultimate sandwich.

Ingredients:

- 3 cups bread flour
- 1 1/2 cups lukewarm water
- 1/4 cup active sourdough starter
- 2 teaspoons salt

Substitutions

- Experiment with adding herbs, olives, or grated cheese to the dough for extra flavor.
- Swap bread flour with a mix of whole wheat and all-purpose flour for a nuttier taste.
- Use a Dutch oven for baking if you don't have a baking stone or sheet.
- Try different types of sourdough starter, like rye or whole wheat, for unique flavor profiles.

Directions

1. In a large bowl, mix bread flour and salt.
2. In a separate bowl, combine lukewarm water and active sourdough starter until dissolved.
3. Gradually add the wet mixture to the dry mixture, stirring until a shaggy dough forms.
4. Cover with a cloth and let the dough rest for 30 minutes.
5. Perform a series of stretch and folds every 30 minutes for the first 2 hours.
6. Cover and let the dough rise for 4-12 hours, or until doubled in size.
7. Preheat your oven to 450°F (232°C) with a baking stone or inverted baking sheet inside.
8. Shape the dough into a round and let it rest on a floured surface.
9. Once the oven is preheated, transfer the dough onto the baking stone or sheet.
10. Score the dough with a sharp knife and bake for about 25-30 minutes, until golden brown and crusty.
11. Let the bread cool before slicing and savoring the taste of the West Coast.
12. Embrace the wild and wonderful world of sourdough!

1
serving

350/se
rving

60
minutes

San Francisco Cioppino

Ingredients:

- 1/4 cup olive oil
- 1 onion, chopped
- 1 bell pepper, chopped
- 2 cloves garlic, minced
- 1 can (28 oz) crushed tomatoes
- 2 cups fish or seafood broth
- 1/2 cup dry white wine
- 1 teaspoon dried oregano
- 1 teaspoon dried basil
- 1/2 teaspoon red pepper flakes
- Salt and black pepper, to taste
- 1 lb mixed seafood (clams, mussels, shrimp, fish fillets)
- Chopped fresh parsley, for garnish
- Sourdough bread, for serving

Substitutions

- Customize the seafood selection based on your preferences and availability.
- Add a pinch of saffron threads for a touch of elegance and color.
- Include diced fennel or celery for extra depth of flavor.
- Use vegetable broth to make a vegetarian version of this hearty stew.
- Serve over cooked pasta or rice for a heartier meal.

A seafood symphony that echoes the Pacific waves, San Francisco Cioppino is a tomato-based stew brimming with the ocean's bounty. With an assortment of fish, shellfish, and aromatic herbs, this dish is a celebration of the sea's flavors. Born in the Italian-American fishing community of San Francisco, it's a culinary testament to the city's coastal heritage.

Directions

1. In a large pot, heat olive oil over medium heat.
2. Add chopped onion and chopped bell pepper. Cook until softened.
3. Stir in minced garlic and cook until fragrant.
4. Add crushed tomatoes, fish or seafood broth, dry white wine, dried oregano, dried basil, red pepper flakes, salt, and black pepper.
5. Bring to a simmer and let flavors meld for about 15-20 minutes.
6. Add mixed seafood to the pot and cook until seafood is cooked through and shellfish have opened, about 5-10 minutes.
7. Discard any unopened shellfish.
8. Ladle the Cioppino into bowls, garnish with chopped fresh parsley, and serve with sourdough bread for dipping.
9. Dive into the rich and savory depths of San Francisco's coastal cuisine.

1 bowl

400/se
rving

30
minutes

Hawaiian Poke Bowl

Ingredients:

- 1 lb sashimi-grade fish (tuna, salmon, or a mix), cubed
- 1/4 cup soy sauce
- 1 tablespoon sesame oil
- 1 teaspoon rice vinegar
- 1 teaspoon ginger, minced
- 1 teaspoon garlic, minced
- 1/2 teaspoon red pepper flakes
- Sliced green onions, for garnish
- Sesame seeds, for garnish
- Avocado slices, cucumber slices, edamame, seaweed salad, and pickled ginger, for topping
- Cooked white or brown rice

A taste of the aloha spirit, Hawaiian Poke Bowl is a colorful and fresh dish that showcases the flavors of the Pacific. Sashimi-grade fish is marinated in a blend of soy sauce, sesame oil, and other aromatics. Served over a bed of rice and accompanied by an array of toppings, this bowl is a delightful journey to the Hawaiian islands. Mahalo for the culinary adventure!

Directions

1. In a bowl, whisk together soy sauce, sesame oil, rice vinegar, minced ginger, minced garlic, and red pepper flakes.
2. Add cubed fish to the marinade and gently toss to coat.
3. Let the fish marinate in the fridge for about 15-20 minutes, allowing the flavors to meld.
4. Assemble the poke bowl by placing a bed of cooked rice in a bowl.
5. Arrange the marinated fish on top of the rice.
6. Garnish with sliced green onions, sesame seeds, avocado slices, cucumber slices, edamame, seaweed salad, and pickled ginger.
7. Drizzle with additional soy sauce or sesame oil, if desired.
8. Experience the vibrant flavors of Hawaii with each bite of this fresh and healthy bowl.

1
serving

350/se
rving

30
minutes

Pacific Northwest Salmon

Ingredients:

- 2 salmon fillets (6 oz each)
- Salt and black pepper, to taste
- 2 tablespoons olive oil
- 2 tablespoons maple syrup
- 1 tablespoon Dijon mustard
- 1 teaspoon dried dill
- Lemon wedges, for serving

Substitutions

- Substitute maple syrup with honey or brown sugar for the glaze.
- Enhance the glaze with minced garlic or grated ginger for an extra kick.
- Grill the salmon on a cedar plank for added smokiness and aroma.
- Top with chopped fresh herbs, like parsley or chives, for a burst of freshness.
- Serve over quinoa or couscous for a wholesome meal.

A Pacific treasure, Pacific Northwest Salmon captures the essence of the region's waters. Fresh salmon fillets are seasoned with herbs, brushed with a maple glaze, and grilled to perfection. With a balance of smokiness and sweetness, this dish embodies the natural beauty of Oregon and Washington. Indulge in the simplicity of flavors from land and sea.

Directions

1. Preheat grill to medium-high heat.
2. Season salmon fillets with salt and black pepper.
3. In a bowl, whisk together olive oil, maple syrup, Dijon mustard, and dried dill.
4. Brush the glaze over the salmon fillets.
5. Grill salmon fillets for about 4-5 minutes per side, or until the salmon flakes easily with a fork.
6. Remove from the grill and let rest for a minute.
7. Squeeze lemon juice over the salmon fillets.
8. Serve with a side of roasted vegetables or a fresh salad.
9. Delight in the taste of the Pacific Northwest's finest catch.

1
serving

300/se
rving

15
minutes

Alaskan King Crab Legs

Ingredients:

- Alaskan King Crab legs
- Melted butter, for dipping

Substitutions

- Sprinkle Old Bay seasoning or lemon pepper on the crab legs before steaming for added flavor.
- Create a garlic herb butter or a spicy chili-lime dipping sauce for a twist.
- Serve with a side of garlic mashed potatoes or a fresh green salad for a complete meal.
- Pair with a crisp white wine or a light beer to complement the delicate flavors.
- Use crab crackers or kitchen shears to make cracking open the crab legs easier.

A regal feast from the icy waters, Alaskan King Crab Legs are a luxurious delicacy that requires minimal effort to enjoy. Steamed to succulent perfection, these crab legs are a celebration of Alaskan bounty. Serve with melted butter for dipping, and let the sweet and tender crab meat transport you to the wild beauty of the Last Frontier.

Directions

1. Steam Alaskan King Crab legs over boiling water for about 5-7 minutes, until the crab meat is heated through.
2. Crack the legs open to reveal the sweet crab meat.
3. Dip the crab meat into melted butter or your favorite dipping sauce.
4. Enjoy the luxurious taste of Alaskan seafood, reminiscent of the pristine waters and rugged landscapes of the region.

1
serving

250/se
rving

45
minutes

Idaho Potato Soup

A comforting embrace from the Gem State, Idaho Potato Soup is a creamy and hearty creation that warms the soul. With velvety potatoes, savory bacon, and a touch of cheese, this soup is the epitome of comfort food. It's a tribute to Idaho's agricultural heritage and a bowl of pure satisfaction, perfect for chasing away the chill of a mountain evening.

Ingredients:

- 4 russet potatoes, peeled and diced
- 4 cups chicken or vegetable broth
- 1 onion, chopped
- 2 cloves garlic, minced
- 4 strips bacon, cooked and crumbled
- 1 cup shredded cheddar cheese
- 1/2 cup heavy cream
- Chopped chives or green onions, for garnish
- Salt and black pepper, to taste

Substitutions

- Add diced carrots or celery to the soup for extra depth of flavor and color.
- Sprinkle with grated Parmesan or smoked paprika for an extra layer of richness.
- Substitute heavy cream with half-and-half or whole milk for a lighter version.
- Top with croutons or crispy fried onions for added texture.
- Serve with a side of crusty bread or buttery dinner rolls for a complete meal.

Directions

1. In a pot, combine diced potatoes, chopped onion, minced garlic, and chicken or vegetable broth.
2. Bring to a boil and let simmer until potatoes are tender, about 15-20 minutes.
3. Use an immersion blender to partially blend the soup, leaving some chunks for texture.
4. Stir in crumbled bacon, shredded cheddar cheese, and heavy cream.
5. Simmer for an additional 10-15 minutes, allowing flavors to meld.
6. Season with salt and black pepper to taste.
7. Ladle the potato soup into bowls and garnish with chopped chives or green onions.
8. Cozy up to the flavors of Idaho with each creamy spoonful.

1
serving

300/se
rving

30
minutes

Rocky Mountain Oysters

Ingredients:

- 4 bull testicles
- 1 cup buttermilk
- 1 cup all-purpose flour
- 1 teaspoon paprika
- Salt and black pepper, to taste
- Vegetable oil, for frying
- Lemon wedges, for serving

Substitutions

- Add a pinch of cayenne pepper or chili powder to the flour mixture for a kick of heat.
- Experiment with different batters, like beer batter or tempura batter, for a twist.
- Serve with a dipping sauce made from mayonnaise and your favorite hot sauce.
- Garnish with chopped fresh herbs, like parsley or cilantro, for a burst of freshness.
- Pair with a cold beer or a bold red wine for a balanced experience.

A brave delight from the mountainous terrain, Rocky Mountain Oysters are a true taste adventure. Also known as "prairie oysters," these are actually bull testicles that are breaded and fried to crispy perfection. A delicacy embraced by the curious and the daring, this dish is a testament to the West's wild spirit and culinary curiosity. Approach with an open mind!

Directions

1. Carefully peel the tough skin from the bull testicles.
2. Slice the testicles into thin rounds.
3. Soak the sliced testicles in buttermilk for about 30 minutes.
4. In a bowl, combine all-purpose flour, paprika, salt, and black pepper.
5. Heat vegetable oil in a deep skillet to 350°F (175°C).
6. Drain the testicle slices from the buttermilk and dredge them in the flour mixture.
7. Fry the testicle slices in the hot oil until golden and crispy, about 2-3 minutes per side.
8. Drain on paper towels.
9. Serve with lemon wedges and embark on a unique culinary journey through the rugged West.
10. Approach with curiosity and an adventurous spirit.

1 taco

350/se
rving

60
minutes

Southwest Navajo Taco

Ingredients:

- For Fry Bread:
  - 2 cups all-purpose flour
  - 2 teaspoons baking powder
  - 1/2 teaspoon salt
  - 3/4 cup warm water
  - Vegetable oil, for frying
- For Topping:
  - 1 lb ground meat (beef, bison, or turkey)
  - 1 packet taco seasoning
  - 1 can (15 oz) refried beans
  - Shredded lettuce, diced tomatoes, diced onions, sliced jalapeños, shredded cheese, sour cream, and salsa, for topping

Directions

For Fry Bread:
1. In a bowl, whisk together flour, baking powder, and salt.
2. Gradually add warm water and knead until a smooth dough forms.
3. Cover and let the dough rest for 30 minutes.
4. Divide the dough into portions and shape each portion into a flat round.
5. Heat vegetable oil in a deep skillet to 375°F (190°C).
6. Fry the dough rounds until puffed and golden, about 2 minutes per side.
7. Drain on paper towels.

For Topping:
1. In a skillet, cook ground meat until browned. Drain excess fat.
2. Stir in taco seasoning and prepare according to packet instructions.
3. Warm refried beans in a saucepan.
4. Assemble the Navajo Tacos by placing a fry bread on a plate.
5. Spread a layer of refried beans on the fry bread.
6. Top with seasoned ground meat, shredded lettuce, diced tomatoes, diced onions, sliced jalapeños, shredded cheese, sour cream, and salsa.
7. Dive into the savory and vibrant flavors of the Southwest.

1
serving

300/se
rving

90
minutes

Santa Fe Green Chile Stew

A symphony of flavors from the Land of Enchantment, Santa Fe Green Chile Stew is a soulful and spicy creation that warms the heart. Roasted green chiles, tender chunks of pork, and hearty potatoes come together in a rich broth. A reflection of New Mexico's vibrant culinary culture, this stew is an invitation to savor the warmth of the Southwest with every spoonful.

Ingredients:

- 1 lb pork shoulder, trimmed and cubed
- Salt and black pepper, to taste
- 2 tablespoons vegetable oil
- 1 onion, chopped
- 2 cloves garlic, minced
- 2 cans (4 oz each) roasted green chiles, chopped
- 3 cups chicken broth
- 2 cups diced potatoes
- 1 teaspoon ground cumin
- 1 teaspoon dried oregano
- Chopped fresh cilantro, for garnish
- Lime wedges, for serving

Substitutions

- Use roasted poblano peppers instead of green chiles for a milder flavor and a touch of smokiness.
- Incorporate diced tomatoes or corn for extra color and texture.
- Add a splash of vinegar or a squeeze of lime juice for a tangy kick.
- Serve with warm tortillas or cornbread for a satisfying meal.
- Top with a dollop of sour cream or a sprinkle of queso fresco for added creaminess.

Directions

1. Season cubed pork with salt and black pepper.
2. In a pot, heat vegetable oil over medium-high heat.
3. Add cubed pork and cook until browned on all sides. Remove from the pot and set aside.
4. In the same pot, add chopped onion and cook until translucent.
5. Stir in minced garlic and cook until fragrant.
6. Add chopped roasted green chiles, cooked pork, chicken broth, diced potatoes, ground cumin, and dried oregano.
7. Bring to a boil and let simmer for about 45-60 minutes, until pork is tender and flavors meld.
8. Ladle the stew into bowls and garnish with chopped fresh cilantro.
9. Serve with lime wedges for a touch of tanginess.
10. Embrace the captivating flavors of Santa Fe and the Southwest.

1 burger

400/se
rving

30
minutes

Wyoming Bison Burger

Ingredients:

- 1/2 lb ground bison meat
- Salt and black pepper, to taste
- 1 teaspoon Worcestershire sauce
- 1/2 teaspoon garlic powder
- Sliced cheese, lettuce, tomato, onion, pickles, and condiments of your choice, for topping
- Burger buns

Substitutions

- Experiment with different types of cheese, such as cheddar, pepper jack, or blue cheese.
- Add crispy bacon or sautéed mushrooms for extra indulgence.
- Create a bison burger sauce using mayonnaise, ketchup, and a touch of hot sauce.
- Grill slices of red onion or bell pepper for a smoky and sweet topping.
- Serve with a side of sweet potato fries or onion rings for a classic pairing.

A tribute to the rugged wilderness, Wyoming Bison Burger is a lean and flavorful take on the classic. Juicy bison meat is seasoned and grilled to perfection, showcasing the unique taste of the West's iconic plains. Topped with your favorite fixings and nestled in a bun, this burger invites you to savor the untamed flavors of the Cowboy State.

Directions

1. In a bowl, gently combine ground bison meat, salt, black pepper, Worcestershire sauce, and garlic powder.
2. Shape the mixture into a patty, slightly larger than the burger bun.
3. Preheat grill to medium-high heat.
4. Grill the bison burger for about 3-4 minutes per side, or until the desired level of doneness is achieved.
5. During the last minute of grilling, place a slice of cheese on the burger patty to melt.
6. Toast the burger buns on the grill for a minute or two.
7. Assemble the Wyoming Bison Burger by placing the cooked patty on the bun.
8. Top with lettuce, tomato, onion, pickles, and your choice of condiments.
9. Sink your teeth into the bold and robust flavors of the untamed West.
10. Savor the essence of Wyoming's wild landscapes and cowboy spirit.

Chapter 5:
Coastal Treasures

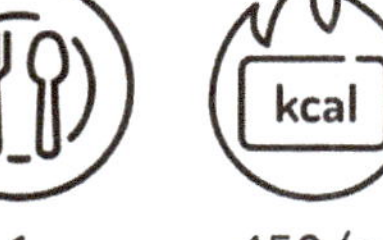

1
sandwic
h

450/se
rving

30
minutes

Philly Cheese Steak

Ingredients:

- 1 lb ribeye or top round beef, thinly sliced
- 2 large onions, thinly sliced
- Salt and black pepper, to taste
- 4 soft hoagie rolls
- 8 slices provolone or American cheese
- Mayonnaise or cheese sauce, for topping

Substitutions

- Customize with bell peppers, mushrooms, or jalapeños for added texture and flavor.
- Try different cheeses, like Cheez Whiz, provolone, or Swiss, for a unique twist.
- Serve with hot or sweet peppers for a spicy kick.
- Swap beef with chicken or seitan for a different take on the classic.
- Add a sprinkle of garlic powder or crushed red pepper flakes for extra zing.

A slice of Philadelphia's culinary legacy, Philly Cheese Steak is an iconic sandwich that's a harmony of flavors. Thinly sliced beefsteak is cooked with onions, topped with gooey melted cheese, and nestled in a soft roll. Whether you're a local or a visitor, this sandwich invites you to taste the heart of the City of Brotherly Love with every bite.

Directions

1. In a skillet, cook the thinly sliced beef over medium-high heat until browned. Season with salt and black pepper.
2. Push the beef to one side of the skillet and add the thinly sliced onions. Cook until onions are soft and caramelized.
3. Mix the beef and onions together, creating a flavorful blend.
4. Split the hoagie rolls and lay cheese slices on one side of each roll.
5. Spoon the beef and onion mixture over the cheese-covered side of the roll.
6. Close the rolls and let the heat from the beef melt the cheese.
7. Serve with mayonnaise or cheese sauce, and take a bite into the savory history of Philadelphia.

1
serving

400/se
rving

120
minutes

New Orleans Gumbo

Ingredients:

- 1/2 cup vegetable oil
- 1/2 cup all-purpose flour
- 1 onion, chopped
- 1 bell pepper, chopped
- 2 celery stalks, chopped
- 3 cloves garlic, minced
- 12 oz smoked sausage, sliced
- 2 boneless chicken breasts, cubed
- 1 lb shrimp, peeled and deveined
- 1 teaspoon Cajun seasoning
- 1 teaspoon dried thyme
- 1 teaspoon dried oregano
- 1/2 teaspoon cayenne pepper
- 4 cups chicken broth
- 1 can (14 oz) diced tomatoes
- 1 cup okra, sliced
- Cooked white rice, for serving
- Chopped green onions and hot sauce, for garnish

A true Cajun masterpiece, New Orleans Gumbo is a celebration of the bayou's flavors. With a rich and hearty base, this stew features an array of ingredients—smoked sausage, chicken, shrimp, and a medley of vegetables—all steeped in a flavorful roux. It's a culinary journey through the streets and soul of the Big Easy, where every spoonful tells a story.

Directions

1. In a pot, heat vegetable oil over medium heat. Add all-purpose flour and stir constantly to create a roux. Cook until roux is a deep brown color, similar to peanut butter.
2. Add chopped onion, chopped bell pepper, chopped celery, and minced garlic to the roux. Cook until vegetables are tender.
3. Stir in sliced smoked sausage and cubed chicken. Cook until chicken is no longer pink.
4. Season with Cajun seasoning, dried thyme, dried oregano, and cayenne pepper.
5. Pour in chicken broth and diced tomatoes. Bring to a simmer.
6. Add sliced okra and peeled shrimp. Let the gumbo simmer for about 45-60 minutes, allowing flavors to meld.
7. Serve the gumbo over cooked white rice, garnished with chopped green onions and a dash of hot sauce.
8. Savor the soulful flavors of New Orleans with every spoonful.

1
serving

300/se
rving

45
minutes

Maryland Crab Cakes

Ingredients:

- 1 lb lump crab meat, picked over for shells
- 1/2 cup mayonnaise
- 1 tablespoon Dijon mustard
- 1 egg, beaten
- 1 teaspoon Old Bay seasoning
- 1 teaspoon Worcestershire sauce
- 1 teaspoon lemon juice
- 1/2 teaspoon salt
- 1/4 teaspoon black pepper
- 1 cup breadcrumbs
- 2 tablespoons butter or vegetable oil, for frying
- Lemon wedges, for serving

Substitutions

- Add finely chopped bell pepper or green onion for added color and freshness.
- Create a remoulade sauce using mayonnaise, mustard, capers, and herbs for dipping.
- Bake the crab cakes in the oven for a lighter version.
- Experiment with different types of crab meat, like snow crab or Dungeness crab, for unique flavors.
- Serve on a bed of mixed greens or with a side of coleslaw for a balanced meal.

A culinary jewel of the Chesapeake Bay, Maryland Crab Cakes showcase the sweet and delicate taste of blue crab meat. With a blend of seasonings and breadcrumbs, these cakes are pan-fried to a golden crisp. Served with a squeeze of lemon, they're a tribute to the coastal bounty and maritime heritage of the Old Line State. Relish the taste of the sea on a plate.

Directions

1. In a bowl, gently combine lump crab meat, mayonnaise, Dijon mustard, beaten egg, Old Bay seasoning, Worcestershire sauce, lemon juice, salt, and black pepper.
2. Gradually fold in breadcrumbs until the mixture holds together.
3. Shape the mixture into crab cakes, about 1/2 inch thick.
4. In a skillet, heat butter or vegetable oil over medium heat.
5. Pan-fry the crab cakes until golden brown and crispy on both sides, about 3-4 minutes per side.
6. Drain on paper towels.
7. Serve with lemon wedges and let the taste of Maryland's coastal waters shine on your palate.

1
serving

350/se
rving

60
minutes

New England Clam Chowder

Ingredients:

- 2 cups chopped clams, fresh or canned
- 2 slices bacon, chopped
- 1 onion, chopped
- 2 celery stalks, chopped
- 2 cups diced potatoes
- 2 cups milk
- 1 cup heavy cream
- 2 tablespoons butter
- 2 tablespoons all-purpose flour
- Salt and black pepper, to taste
- Chopped fresh parsley, for garnish
- Oyster crackers, for serving

Substitutions

- Include corn kernels or diced carrots for added sweetness and texture.
- Garnish with crumbled oyster crackers for extra crunch.
- Use half-and-half or whole milk for a lighter version of the chowder.
- Add a pinch of thyme or a bay leaf for an extra layer of flavor.
- Serve in bread bowls for a fun presentation and a hearty meal.

Directions

1. If using fresh clams, steam them until they open. Reserve the clam meat and juice.
2. In a pot, cook chopped bacon until crispy. Remove bacon and set aside.
3. In the same pot, melt butter. Add chopped onion and chopped celery. Cook until vegetables are softened.
4. Stir in all-purpose flour and cook for a minute to create a roux.
5. Gradually add milk and heavy cream, stirring to combine.
6. Add diced potatoes and the reserved clam juice. Bring to a simmer and cook until potatoes are tender.
7. Gently fold in chopped clams and crispy bacon. Simmer for a few minutes to heat through.
8. Season with salt and black pepper.
9. Ladle the clam chowder into bowls, garnish with chopped fresh parsley, and serve with oyster crackers.
10. Enjoy the rich and briny flavors of New England's coastal charm.

1
serving

250/se
rving

60
minutes

Chesapeake Bay Blue Crabs

Ingredients:

- Live blue crabs
- Water
- Apple cider vinegar
- Old Bay seasoning
- Melted butter, for dipping
- Bibs, mallets, and plenty of napkins

Substitutions

- Enhance the flavor by adding whole cloves of garlic, lemon slices, or whole peppercorns to the boiling water.
- Add corn on the cob and red potatoes to the steaming pot for a complete crab boil.
- Dip the crab meat in garlic aioli or a tangy cocktail sauce for variety.
- Serve with a side of coleslaw and freshly baked bread to complete the meal.
- Enjoy outdoors for the full crab boil experience.

An emblem of Maryland's maritime culture, Chesapeake Bay Blue Crabs are a coastal treasure that beckons with their sweet and succulent meat. Steamed to perfection with a blend of spices, these crabs are a hands-on feast that demands your full attention. Crack open the shells and savor the taste of the bay and the camaraderie of a crab feast.

Directions

1. Fill a large pot with water and add apple cider vinegar. Bring to a boil.
2. Add a generous amount of Old Bay seasoning to the boiling water.
3. Carefully place live blue crabs into the pot. Cover and steam for about 20-30 minutes, until the crabs turn bright red.
4. Using tongs, transfer the steamed crabs to a large tray or platter.
5. Serve the Chesapeake Bay Blue Crabs with melted butter for dipping, along with bibs, mallets, and lots of napkins.
6. Gather friends and family for a crab feast and savor the communal joy of cracking crabs together.

1 slice

300/se
rving

45
minutes

Florida Key Lime Pie

Ingredients:

- For Graham Cracker Crust:
  - 1 1/2 cups graham cracker crumbs
  - 1/4 cup sugar
  - 1/2 cup unsalted butter, melted
- For Key Lime Filling:
  - 4 large egg yolks
  - 2 cans (14 oz each) sweetened condensed milk
  - 1/2 cup key lime juice
  - Zest of 2 key limes
- Whipped cream and lime slices, for garnish

Substitutions

- Substitute regular limes if key limes are unavailable, but adjust the quantity for a more intense flavor.
- Top with a drizzle of raspberry or passion fruit sauce for an extra layer of fruity goodness.
- Create a coconut graham cracker crust for a tropical twist.
- Serve with a scoop of coconut or mango sorbet for a refreshing pairing.
- Enjoy with a glass of iced tea or a coconut-infused cocktail for a true taste of Florida.

Directions

For Graham Cracker Crust:
1. Preheat the oven to 350°F (175°C).
2. In a bowl, mix graham cracker crumbs, sugar, and melted butter until well combined.
3. Press the mixture into a pie dish, forming an even crust along the bottom and sides.
4. Bake the crust for about 10 minutes, until golden brown. Let cool.

For Key Lime Filling:
1. In a bowl, whisk egg yolks until smooth.
2. Gradually whisk in sweetened condensed milk, key lime juice, and key lime zest until well combined.
3. Pour the filling into the cooled crust.
4. Bake the pie for about 15-20 minutes, until the filling is set but still slightly jiggly in the center.
5. Let the pie cool to room temperature, then refrigerate for a few hours or overnight.
6. Garnish with whipped cream and lime slices before serving.
7. Revel in the zesty sweetness of Florida's tropical charm with each luscious bite.

1
serving

450/se
rving

60
minutes

Low Country Boil

Ingredients:

- 1 lb large shrimp, unpeeled
- 1 lb crab clusters
- 4 smoked sausages, sliced
- 6 ears corn, shucked and halved
- 1 lb red potatoes, halved
- 1 onion, quartered
- 4 cloves garlic, smashed
- 2 lemons, halved
- 2 tablespoons Old Bay seasoning
- 1 tablespoon Cajun seasoning
- 1 teaspoon red pepper flakes (optional)
- Cocktail sauce and melted butter, for dipping
- Fresh parsley, for garnish
- Newspaper, for serving

Substitutions

- Include crawfish, mussels, or clams for a diverse seafood experience.
- Substitute smoked sausage with spicy andouille sausage for extra heat.
- Add sliced leeks or celery for added depth of flavor.
- Experiment with different dipping sauces, like garlic aioli or remoulade.
- Serve with a side of coleslaw or potato salad to complement the feast.

A communal feast from the Carolina coast, Low Country Boil is a joyful medley of seafood, sausage, and vegetables. Shrimp, crab, corn, and potatoes are boiled together with a blend of spices, creating a delightful burst of flavors. Spread out the feast on a newspaper-covered table, and savor the camaraderie and coastal spirit of the Low Country.

Directions

1. Fill a large pot with water and add Old Bay seasoning, Cajun seasoning, and red pepper flakes (if using).
2. Squeeze lemon juice into the water and add the lemon halves.
3. Bring the seasoned water to a boil.
4. Add halved potatoes and cook for about 10-15 minutes, until slightly tender.
5. Add sliced sausages, quartered onion, smashed garlic, and halved corn. Cook for an additional 10 minutes.
6. Add crab clusters and unpeeled shrimp. Cook for about 3-5 minutes, until the shrimp turn pink and the crab is heated through.
7. Drain the boil and spread the feast on a newspaper-covered table.
8. Garnish with chopped fresh parsley.
9. Serve with cocktail sauce and melted butter for dipping.
10. Gather friends and family, and revel in the communal delight of the Low Country Boil.

1
serving

300/se
rving

240
minutes

Hawaiian Luau Kalua Pork

Ingredients:

- 4 lb pork shoulder, bone-in
- 2 tablespoons sea salt
- Banana leaves or aluminum foil
- Pineapple slices, for garnish
- Fresh cilantro, for garnish
- Cooked white rice, for serving

Substitutions

- Create a marinade using soy sauce, ginger, garlic, and brown sugar for an extra layer of flavor.
- Add a drizzle of teriyaki sauce or a sprinkle of toasted sesame seeds for a touch of Asian-inspired goodness.
- Serve with macaroni salad and poi for a traditional Hawaiian plate lunch.
- Enjoy with a tropical fruit punch or a coconut water cocktail to complete the island experience.
- Play Hawaiian music and imagine yourself on a sun-kissed beach.

A taste of the tropics, Hawaiian Luau Kalua Pork is a succulent dish slow-cooked to perfection. Seasoned with sea salt and wrapped in banana leaves, the pork absorbs the smoky flavors of the imu (underground oven). With every tender bite, you'll be transported to the lush landscapes and vibrant culture of the Hawaiian Islands. Aloha in every mouthful.

Directions

1. Preheat your oven to 325°F (165°C).
2. Rub sea salt all over the pork shoulder, ensuring even coverage.
3. Wrap the pork tightly in banana leaves or aluminum foil.
4. Place the wrapped pork in a roasting pan and roast in the preheated oven for about 4 hours, until the pork is tender and easily shreds with a fork.
5. Unwrap the pork and shred it using two forks. Discard any excess fat and bones.
6. Serve the Kalua Pork over cooked white rice, garnished with pineapple slices and chopped fresh cilantro.
7. Savor the tropical flavors and the spirit of aloha in each mouthful of this Hawaiian delight.

1
serving

300/se
rving

45
minutes

West Coast Dungeness Crab

Ingredients:

- Live Dungeness crab
- Water
- White wine
- Bay leaves
- Drawn butter, for dipping
- Bibs, crackers, and plenty of napkins

Substitutions
- Enhance the flavor by adding a few lemon slices, garlic cloves, or a sprinkle of red pepper flakes to the boiling water.
- Serve with a side of coleslaw or a fresh green salad to balance the richness of the crab.
- Enjoy with a chilled glass of white wine or a light and crisp lager to complement the flavors.
- Delight in the sunset while savoring each succulent bite of the crab.
- Create a beach-themed ambiance with seashells and ocean sounds for a true coastal dining experience.

A Pacific delicacy, West Coast Dungeness Crab is a delectable treat that showcases the bounty of the ocean. Steamed and served with drawn butter, this crab offers tender and sweet meat that's a delight to crack open and savor. Transport yourself to the rugged beauty of the Pacific coastline as you relish the taste of this coastal treasure.

Directions

1. Fill a large pot with water and add white wine and bay leaves for flavor.
2. Bring the seasoned water to a boil.
3. Gently place live Dungeness crab into the pot. Cover and steam for about 15-20 minutes, until the crab turns a vibrant red color.
4. Using tongs, transfer the steamed crab to a large tray or platter.
5. Serve the West Coast Dungeness Crab with drawn butter for dipping, along with bibs, crackers, and plenty of napkins.
6. Embrace the flavors of the Pacific coastline and let the taste of the sea take you on a culinary journey.

2 tacos

350/se
rving

30
minutes

Pacific Coast Fish Tacos

Ingredients:

- 1 lb white fish fillets (such as cod or halibut)
- 1 cup all-purpose flour
- 1 teaspoon paprika
- Salt and black pepper, to taste
- Vegetable oil, for frying
- 8 small flour tortillas
- 2 cups coleslaw mix (cabbage and carrots)
- 1/4 cup mayonnaise
- 1 tablespoon lime juice
- 1 teaspoon honey
- 1 cup salsa, store-bought or homemade
- Fresh cilantro, for garnish
- Lime wedges, for serving

Substitutions

- Customize the slaw by adding diced avocado, red onion, or jicama for extra crunch and flavor.
- Experiment with different types of fish, like mahi-mahi or snapper, based on availability.
- Drizzle with a creamy chipotle sauce or a tangy yogurt-based dressing for added depth.
- Serve with a side of black beans or Mexican rice to complete the meal.
- Listen to surf music or watch a beach sunset while savoring the deliciousness.

A fusion of flavors inspired by the Pacific coast, Pacific Coast Fish Tacos are a celebration of fresh seafood and vibrant produce. Crispy fish fillets are nestled in warm tortillas and topped with a medley of colorful slaw and zesty salsa. With every bite, you'll taste the ocean breeze and the coastal spirit that defines the West Coast culinary scene.

Directions

1. In a bowl, mix all-purpose flour, paprika, salt, and black pepper.
2. Dredge fish fillets in the flour mixture, shaking off excess.
3. In a skillet, heat vegetable oil over medium-high heat.
4. Fry fish fillets until golden and crispy, about 2-3 minutes per side. Drain on paper towels.
5. In a separate bowl, combine coleslaw mix, mayonnaise, lime juice, and honey. Toss to coat.
6. Warm flour tortillas in a dry skillet or microwave.
7. Assemble the Pacific Coast Fish Tacos by placing a crispy fish fillet in each tortilla.
8. Top with a generous spoonful of coleslaw mixture and salsa.
9. Garnish with fresh cilantro and serve with lime wedges.
10. Enjoy the vibrant flavors and the coastal charm of the West Coast.

Chapter 6:
Heartland Classics

1
serving

450/se
rving

240
minutes

Kansas City BBQ Ribs

A barbecue masterpiece from the heart of Missouri, Kansas City BBQ Ribs are tender, smoky, and slathered in a rich tomato-based sauce. With a perfect balance of sweet and tangy flavors, each bite is a journey to the world of BBQ bliss. Savor the slow-cooked perfection that embodies the essence of the Heartland.

Ingredients:

- 2 racks baby back ribs
- 1/4 cup brown sugar
- 2 tablespoons paprika
- 1 tablespoon black pepper
- 1 tablespoon salt
- 1 tablespoon chili powder
- 1 tablespoon garlic powder
- 1 tablespoon onion powder
- 1 teaspoon cayenne pepper (adjust to taste)
- 1 cup Kansas City-style barbecue sauce
- Apple wood chips, soaked in water
- Coleslaw, for serving
- Cornbread, for serving
- Pickles and onions, for garnish

Directions

1. Prepare the ribs by removing the membrane from the back.
2. In a bowl, mix brown sugar, paprika, black pepper, salt, chili powder, garlic powder, onion powder, and cayenne pepper to create a dry rub.
3. Rub the dry rub all over the ribs, covering both sides.
4. Preheat your smoker or grill for indirect heat at around 225°F (110°C).
5. Add soaked apple wood chips for a smoky flavor.
6. Place the ribs on the smoker or grill, bone-side down, and cook for about 3 hours.
7. Baste the ribs with Kansas City-style barbecue sauce and cook for an additional 30 minutes, until the ribs are tender and glazed.
8. Slice the ribs between the bones and serve with coleslaw, cornbread, pickles, and onions.
9. Let the flavors of Kansas City BBQ Ribs transport you to a world of barbecue perfection.

1
serving

500/se
rving

60
minutes

Oklahoma Indian Tacos

Ingredients:

- For Fry Bread:
  - 2 cups all-purpose flour
  - 1 tablespoon baking powder
  - 1/2 teaspoon salt
  - 1 cup warm water
  - Vegetable oil, for frying
- For Taco Toppings:
  - 1 lb ground beef or bison
  - 1 packet taco seasoning
  - 1 can (15 oz) pinto beans, drained and rinsed
  - Shredded lettuce
  - Diced tomatoes
  - Shredded cheddar cheese
  - Sour cream
  - Sliced jalapeños
  - Chopped fresh cilantro
- Salsa or hot sauce, for drizzling

Directions

For Fry Bread:
1. In a bowl, mix all-purpose flour, baking powder, and salt.
2. Gradually add warm water and knead the dough until smooth.
3. Divide the dough into small balls and flatten into rounds.
4. In a skillet, heat vegetable oil over medium-high heat.
5. Fry the dough rounds until golden brown and puffed.
6. Drain on paper towels.

For Taco Toppings:
1. In a skillet, cook ground beef or bison until browned. Drain excess fat.
2. Add taco seasoning and water, following packet instructions.
3. Warm pinto beans in a separate pot.
4. To assemble, place a fry bread round on a plate.
5. Top with seasoned meat, beans, lettuce, tomatoes, cheese, sour cream, jalapeños, and cilantro.
6. Drizzle with salsa or hot sauce.
7. Embrace the fusion of flavors and cultures with each Oklahoma Indian Taco you enjoy.

1
serving

400/se
rving

120
minutes

Texas Chili

Ingredients:

- 2 lb beef chuck roast, cubed
- 2 tablespoons vegetable oil
- 1 onion, chopped
- 3 cloves garlic, minced
- 2 tablespoons chili powder
- 1 teaspoon cumin
- 1 teaspoon paprika
- 1/2 teaspoon cayenne pepper (adjust to taste)
- 1 can (14 oz) diced tomatoes
- 2 cups beef broth
- Salt and black pepper, to taste
- Chopped fresh cilantro, for garnish
- Shredded cheddar cheese, for garnish
- Sour cream, for garnish
- Sliced jalapeños, for garnish

A Lone Star State classic, Texas Chili is a bold and robust stew that's all about the meat and spices. With chunks of tender beef, a rich chili sauce, and a touch of heat, each spoonful is a tribute to the cowboy spirit and the flavors of the Southwest. Let the warmth of the chili and the heartiness of the beef take you on a culinary journey to the open prairies.

Directions

1. In a pot, heat vegetable oil over medium-high heat.
2. Add cubed beef and cook until browned on all sides. Remove beef and set aside.
3. In the same pot, sauté chopped onion and minced garlic until softened.
4. Add chili powder, cumin, paprika, and cayenne pepper. Cook for a minute to release flavors.
5. Return the browned beef to the pot and add diced tomatoes, beef broth, salt, and black pepper.
6. Bring the mixture to a boil, then reduce heat to low and cover.
7. Simmer for about 1.5-2 hours, until the beef is tender and the flavors meld.
8. Serve the Texas Chili hot, garnished with chopped fresh cilantro, shredded cheddar cheese, sour cream, and sliced jalapeños.
9. Let the hearty flavors of Texas fill your heart with cowboy spirit.

1
serving

350/se
rving

45
minutes

South Dakota Chislic

Ingredients:

- 1 lb lamb or beef, cubed
- 2 tablespoons vegetable oil
- 2 cloves garlic, minced
- 1 teaspoon cayenne pepper (adjust to taste)
- Salt and black pepper, to taste
- Sliced white bread
- Butter, for spreading
- Chopped fresh parsley, for garnish
- Lemon wedges, for serving

Substitutions

- Experiment with different marinades using herbs, spices, and citrus juices for diverse flavor profiles.
- Serve with a side of ranch dressing or tzatziki sauce for dipping.
- Use pita bread or flatbread instead of sliced white bread for a twist.
- Enjoy with a glass of local craft beer or a classic root beer float for a refreshing pairing.
- Listen to folk music or Midwestern ballads while savoring the Chislic to fully embrace the Heartland ambiance.

A hidden gem from the Great Plains, South Dakota Chislic is a tantalizing appetizer that's simple yet flavorful. Tender cubes of meat, typically lamb or beef, are marinated, skewered, and grilled to perfection. Served with garlic toast and a dash of cayenne, this dish showcases the warmth of the Heartland's hospitality and taste.

Directions

1. In a bowl, combine cubed meat, vegetable oil, minced garlic, cayenne pepper, salt, and black pepper. Toss to coat.
2. Marinate for about 30 minutes to an hour.
3. Thread marinated meat onto skewers.
4. Preheat the grill to medium-high heat.
5. Grill the skewers for about 5-7 minutes, turning occasionally, until the meat is cooked to your desired doneness.
6. While the meat is grilling, spread butter on slices of white bread and toast on the grill.
7. Sprinkle the toasted bread with chopped fresh parsley.
8. Serve the Chislic skewers hot, accompanied by garlic toast and lemon wedges.
9. Let the simple flavors and hearty goodness of South Dakota Chislic warm your heart.

1
serving

350/se
rving

30
minutes

Iowa Corned Beef Hash

Ingredients:

- 2 cups cooked corned beef, chopped
- 2 cups cooked potatoes, diced
- 1 onion, chopped
- 2 cloves garlic, minced
- Salt and black pepper, to taste
- Butter or oil, for cooking
- Chopped fresh parsley, for garnish
- Fried or poached eggs, for serving

Substitutions

- Add bell peppers or bell pepper for extra color and flavor.
- Top with a dollop of sour cream or a drizzle of hot sauce for added richness and kick.
- Use leftover roasted or boiled potatoes if available.
- Enjoy with a side of buttered toast or fluffy biscuits for a complete breakfast experience.
- Listen to folk or country music while enjoying your meal to enhance the Heartland ambiance.

An Iowa favorite, Corned Beef Hash is a hearty and satisfying dish that transforms leftover corned beef into a comforting meal. Paired with potatoes, onions, and a touch of seasoning, this dish embodies the resourcefulness and warmth of Heartland cooking. As you savor each bite, you'll feel the embrace of Iowa's culinary traditions.

Directions

1. In a skillet, heat butter or oil over medium heat.
2. Sauté chopped onion and minced garlic until softened.
3. Add diced potatoes and cook until they start to brown and crisp.
4. Stir in chopped corned beef and cook until heated through.
5. Season with salt and black pepper to taste.
6. Serve the Iowa Corned Beef Hash hot, garnished with chopped fresh parsley.
7. Top with fried or poached eggs for a classic combination.
8. Let the flavors of Iowa's heartwarming cuisine envelop you with every bite.

1
serving

300/se
rving

45
minutes

Michigan Coney Island Hot Dog

Ingredients:

- For Coney Island Chili Sauce:
 - 1 lb ground beef
 - 1 onion, chopped
 - 2 cloves garlic, minced
 - 2 tablespoons chili powder
 - 1 teaspoon ground cumin
 - 1 teaspoon paprika
 - 1/2 teaspoon ground mustard
 - 1/2 teaspoon allspice
 - 1/4 teaspoon cayenne pepper (adjust to taste)
 - 1 can (14 oz) tomato sauce
 - 1/2 cup beef broth
 - Salt and black pepper, to taste
- For Serving:
 - Hot dog buns
 - Beef hot dogs
 - Diced onions
 - Yellow mustard
 - Shredded cheddar cheese, for topping

A Michigan tradition that's stood the test of time, Coney Island Hot Dogs are a savory delight that pays homage to the vibrant food culture of the Heartland. Topped with a meaty chili sauce, diced onions, and a drizzle of mustard, each bite is a burst of flavor and nostalgia. Experience the iconic taste that's been a cornerstone of Michigan's culinary identity.

Directions

For Coney Island Chili Sauce:
1. In a skillet, cook ground beef over medium heat until browned. Drain excess fat.
2. Add chopped onion and minced garlic. Sauté until onion is translucent.
3. Stir in chili powder, ground cumin, paprika, ground mustard, allspice, and cayenne pepper.
4. Add tomato sauce and beef broth. Simmer for about 15-20 minutes, until the flavors meld.
5. Season with salt and black pepper to taste.

For Serving:
1. Grill or cook beef hot dogs according to package instructions.
2. Place a hot dog in a bun and top with a generous spoonful of Coney Island Chili Sauce.
3. Add diced onions, a drizzle of yellow mustard, and shredded cheddar cheese.
4. Savor the taste of Michigan's culinary legacy with each Coney Island Hot Dog you enjoy.

2
candies

250/se
rving

60
minutes

Ohio Buckeye Candy

Ingredients:

- 1 1/2 cups creamy peanut butter
- 1/2 cup unsalted butter, softened
- 1 teaspoon vanilla extract
- 4 cups powdered sugar
- 2 cups semi-sweet chocolate chips
- 2 tablespoons vegetable shortening
- Toothpicks or skewers

Substitutions

- Use almond butter or cashew butter for a nutty variation on the traditional recipe.
- Add a sprinkle of sea salt on top of the chocolate coating for a sweet and salty contrast.
- Decorate the tops with a drizzle of white chocolate or colored candy melts for a festive touch.
- Package the candies in a decorative tin or box for a delightful homemade gift.
- Listen to folk tunes or Heartland radio stations while enjoying the candies to fully embrace the Ohio ambiance.

Directions

1. In a bowl, mix creamy peanut butter, softened unsalted butter, and vanilla extract until well combined.
2. Gradually add powdered sugar, mixing until a dough forms.
3. Roll the dough into small peanut butter balls, about 1 inch in diameter.
4. Place the peanut butter balls on a baking sheet lined with parchment paper.
5. Insert toothpicks or skewers into the center of each peanut butter ball.
6. Freeze the peanut butter balls for about 30 minutes to firm up.
7. In a microwave-safe bowl, melt chocolate chips and vegetable shortening in 30-second intervals, stirring until smooth.
8. Dip each peanut butter ball into the melted chocolate, leaving a small portion undipped to resemble a "buckeye."
9. Place the dipped candies back on the parchment paper and remove the toothpicks or skewers.
10. Refrigerate the Buckeye Candies until the chocolate is set.
11. Indulge in the creamy and chocolatey goodness of Ohio's beloved confection.

1 slice

350/se
rving

120
minutes

Missouri St. Louis-style Pizza

Ingredients:

- For Pizza Crust:
  - 2 1/4 teaspoons active dry yeast
  - 1 teaspoon sugar
  - 3/4 cup warm water
  - 2 cups all-purpose flour
  - 1 teaspoon salt
- For Pizza Topping:
  - 1 cup Provel cheese, shredded (or blend of white cheddar, Swiss, and provolone)
  - 1/2 cup pizza sauce
  - 1 teaspoon dried oregano
  - Optional toppings: sliced pepperoni, green peppers, onions, black olives
- Olive oil, for brushing
- Grated Parmesan cheese, for garnish

Directions

For Pizza Crust:
1. In a bowl, combine active dry yeast, sugar, and warm water. Let it sit for about 5 minutes until foamy.
2. Mix in all-purpose flour and salt to create a dough.
3. Knead the dough until smooth and elastic, then let it rise in a warm place for about 1 hour.
4. Preheat your oven to 475°F (245°C).
5. Roll out the dough into a thin, rectangular shape on a baking sheet.
6. For Pizza Topping:
1. Sprinkle the shredded Provel cheese over the pizza dough.
2. Dollop pizza sauce over the cheese, then sprinkle dried oregano.
3. Add any desired toppings, such as pepperoni, green peppers, onions, and black olives.
4. Brush the exposed edges of the crust with olive oil.
5. Bake the pizza for about 12-15 minutes, until the crust is crisp and the cheese is bubbly and golden.
6. Sprinkle grated Parmesan cheese over the hot pizza.
7. Immerse yourself in the unique flavors and culinary innovation of Missouri's beloved St. Louis-style Pizza.

1 steak

400/serving

30 minutes

Nebraska Steaks

Ingredients:

- Thick-cut beef steaks (such as ribeye, New York strip, or sirloin)
- Salt and black pepper, to taste
- Olive oil or butter, for cooking
- Fresh herbs (rosemary, thyme, or parsley), for garnish
- Mashed potatoes or buttered corn, for serving

Substitutions

- Infuse the steaks with garlic and herbs by adding minced garlic, chopped rosemary, or thyme leaves during cooking.
- Create a compound butter with herbs and spices to melt over the hot steaks for extra flavor.
- Serve with a side of sautéed green beans or roasted root vegetables to round out the meal.
- Pair with a glass of bold red wine or a locally brewed craft beer to enhance the dining experience.
- Listen to country or folk music while enjoying your steak to fully embrace the Heartland ambiance.

A quintessential Heartland dish, Nebraska Steaks celebrate the Midwest's love for quality beef. A well-seasoned steak is seared to perfection, allowing the natural flavors of the meat to shine. Paired with simple sides, this dish embodies the essence of Nebraska's agrarian roots and culinary pride. Savor the beefy goodness that defines the Heartland.

Directions

1. Preheat a cast-iron skillet or grill pan over high heat.
2. Season the steaks generously with salt and black pepper.
3. Drizzle olive oil or melt butter in the skillet.
4. Add the steaks to the hot skillet and sear for about 3-5 minutes on each side, depending on the desired level of doneness.
5. Use a meat thermometer to gauge the internal temperature (145°F for medium-rare, 160°F for medium, 170°F for well-done).
6. Remove the steaks from the skillet and let them rest for a few minutes.
7. Garnish with fresh herbs.
8. Serve the Nebraska Steaks hot, accompanied by creamy mashed potatoes or buttered corn.
9. Experience the true taste of Heartland beef and the pride of Nebraska's culinary heritage with every succulent bite.

1
serving

300/se
rving

45
minutes

Wisconsin Cheese Soup

Ingredients:

- 1/4 cup unsalted butter
- 1 onion, chopped
- 2 carrots, diced
- 2 celery stalks, diced
- 1/4 cup all-purpose flour
- 2 cups chicken or vegetable broth
- 2 cups whole milk
- 2 cups shredded sharp cheddar cheese
- Salt and white pepper, to taste
- Pinch of nutmeg
- Crumbled cooked bacon, for garnish
- Chopped fresh chives, for garnish

Substitutions

- Add diced potatoes or broccoli florets for added texture and heartiness.
- Garnish with a dollop of sour cream or a drizzle of truffle oil for a luxurious touch.
- Serve with crusty bread or warm pretzels for dipping.
- Enjoy with a glass of creamy milk or a classic root beer float for a nostalgic pairing.
- Listen to folk tunes or old-time radio shows while savoring the soup to fully embrace the Wisconsin ambiance.

Directions

1. In a pot, melt unsalted butter over medium heat.
2. Add chopped onion, diced carrots, and diced celery. Sauté until vegetables are tender.
3. Stir in all-purpose flour to create a roux, cooking for a minute to eliminate the raw flour taste.
4. Gradually add chicken or vegetable broth and whole milk, stirring constantly to prevent lumps.
5. Bring the mixture to a simmer and let it thicken.
6. Reduce heat to low and gradually add shredded sharp cheddar cheese, stirring until melted and smooth.
7. Season with salt, white pepper, and a pinch of nutmeg for depth of flavor.
8. Serve the Wisconsin Cheese Soup hot, garnished with crumbled cooked bacon and chopped fresh chives.
9. Experience the comfort of Wisconsin's dairy heritage with each velvety spoonful.

We need your support

In the midst of this book, we'd like to take a moment to ask for your feedback. Reviews are a precious commodity for us, especially as a small publisher. If you can spare a few moments, we kindly encourage you to return to the app or platform where you made your purchase and click on the review button.

Your rating and a short sentence about your experience with the book would mean the world to us. These reviews can make a significant difference in our journey, as they help us reach more readers. We genuinely appreciate and read each and every review we receive.

Now, let's get back to exploring these delicious recipes!

Chapter 7:
American Fusion

1
chimich
anga

450/se
rving

60
minutes

Tex-Mex Chimichanga

Ingredients:

- 1 lb cooked chicken, shredded (or ground beef)
- 1 cup cooked black beans
- 1 cup cooked rice
- 1 cup shredded cheese (cheddar or Monterey Jack)
- 1 cup salsa or enchilada sauce
- 4 large flour tortillas
- Vegetable oil, for frying
- Sour cream, for topping
- Guacamole, for topping
- Sliced green onions, for garnish
- Chopped fresh cilantro, for garnish

Substitutions

- Customize the filling with sautéed peppers, onions, and corn for added flavor and color.
- Use flour tortillas or whole wheat tortillas based on your preference.
- Opt for vegan cheese and omit dairy-based toppings for a plant-based version.
- Serve with a side of Mexican rice or black bean salad to complement the dish.
- Listen to mariachi music or Tex-Mex tunes while savoring the chimichangas to fully embrace the Southwest ambiance.

A zesty creation from the deserts of Arizona, the Tex-Mex Chimichanga combines the best of both worlds: the crunch of a burrito and the indulgence of deep-fried goodness. Stuffed with savory fillings and topped with cheese, guacamole, and sour cream, this dish is a culinary fusion that's as bold and vibrant as the American Southwest.

Directions

1. In a bowl, combine cooked chicken, cooked black beans, cooked rice, and shredded cheese.
2. Lay out a flour tortilla and spoon the filling mixture onto the center.
3. Fold in the sides and roll up the tortilla to enclose the filling.
4. Secure the ends with toothpicks or kitchen twine.
5. Heat vegetable oil in a deep skillet or pot to about 350°F (175°C).
6. Carefully place the chimichangas in the hot oil and fry until golden brown and crispy.
7. Remove from the oil and drain on paper towels.
8. Top each chimichanga with salsa or enchilada sauce, sour cream, guacamole, sliced green onions, and chopped fresh cilantro.
9. Experience the burst of flavors and textures that define the Tex-Mex Chimichanga.

1
serving

500/se
rving

45
minutes

Hawaiian Plate Lunch

Ingredients:

- 1 cup cooked white rice
- 1 scoop macaroni salad
- 1 serving of cooked protein (chicken, pork, or fish)
- Shoyu sauce or teriyaki sauce, for drizzling
- Sliced fresh pineapple, for garnish
- Chopped fresh parsley, for garnish

Substitutions
- Customize the plate with different proteins and sauces to create your unique combination.
- Add a scoop of creamy potato salad or poi for a traditional touch.
- Enjoy with a glass of refreshing pineapple juice or a tropical fruit smoothie.
- Embrace the island ambiance by listening to Hawaiian music or watching hula dance performances as you savor the plate lunch.

A culinary reflection of Hawaii's cultural diversity, the Hawaiian Plate Lunch is a harmonious blend of flavors and influences. A scoop of rice, macaroni salad, and a protein (like chicken, pork, or fish) come together to create a satisfying and hearty meal that's both comforting and vibrant. Immerse yourself in the aloha spirit with each bite.

Directions

1. Prepare a scoop of cooked white rice and a scoop of macaroni salad on a plate.
2. Add a serving of your preferred cooked protein (chicken, pork, or fish) alongside the rice and macaroni salad.
3. Drizzle the protein with shoyu sauce or teriyaki sauce for an extra layer of flavor.
4. Garnish with sliced fresh pineapple and chopped fresh parsley.
5. Savor the blend of flavors that embodies the spirit of Hawaii's melting pot cuisine.

1
serving

400/se
rving

60
minutes

Cajun Jambalaya

Ingredients:

- 1 cup cooked rice
- 1/2 lb andouille sausage, sliced
- 1/2 lb boneless chicken, diced
- 1 onion, chopped
- 1 green bell pepper, chopped
- 1 celery stalk, chopped
- 2 cloves garlic, minced
- 1 can (14 oz) diced tomatoes
- 1 cup chicken broth
- 1 teaspoon Cajun seasoning
- 1/2 teaspoon paprika
- Pinch of cayenne pepper (adjust to taste)
- Chopped fresh parsley, for garnish

Substitutions

- Include shrimp or crawfish tails for a seafood twist on the classic jambalaya.
- Adjust the level of cayenne pepper to your preferred level of spiciness.
- Serve with a side of buttery cornbread or flaky biscuits to round out the meal.
- Pair with a glass of sweet tea or a classic hurricane cocktail for an authentic experience.
- Listen to zydeco music or jazz tunes while savoring the jambalaya to fully embrace the Louisiana ambiance.

A symphony of flavors from the bayous of Louisiana, Cajun Jambalaya is a rich and hearty dish that captures the essence of Creole cuisine. With a medley of spicy andouille sausage, tender chicken, and vibrant vegetables, each bite is a celebration of Louisiana's unique culinary heritage. Let the flavors of the bayou transport you to the heart of Creole culture.

Directions

1. In a skillet, sauté sliced andouille sausage until browned. Remove and set aside.
2. In the same skillet, cook diced chicken until browned. Remove and set aside.
3. Sauté chopped onion, chopped green bell pepper, chopped celery, and minced garlic until softened.
4. Add diced tomatoes, chicken broth, Cajun seasoning, paprika, and cayenne pepper.
5. Let the mixture simmer for about 10 minutes to meld the flavors.
6. Add the cooked andouille sausage and diced chicken back to the skillet.
7. Serve the jambalaya over cooked rice, garnished with chopped fresh parsley.
8. Let the bold flavors and cultural richness of Louisiana's cuisine come alive with each spoonful.

1
serving

350/se
rving

30
minutes

Detroit Coney Dog

Ingredients:

- Beef hot dog
- Hot dog bun
- 1/2 cup Coney Island Chili Sauce (see Missouri St. Louis-style Pizza recipe)
- Diced onions, for topping
- Yellow mustard, for topping
- Shredded cheddar cheese, for topping

Substitutions

- Customize the toppings with sliced pickles, jalapeños, or a sprinkle of celery salt for added complexity.
- Serve with a side of seasoned waffle fries or onion rings for a classic diner experience.
- Enjoy with a refreshing Vernors ginger ale or a Detroit-made craft beer.
- Listen to Motown classics or Detroit rock tunes while enjoying your Coney Dog to fully embrace the Motor City vibe.

A Detroit original, the Coney Dog is a beloved classic that combines a juicy hot dog with flavorful chili sauce, diced onions, and a squiggle of mustard. Topped with a generous sprinkle of cheddar cheese, this hot dog is a nod to the Motor City's culinary ingenuity and passion for comfort food. Experience the taste of Detroit with every bite.

Directions

1. Grill or cook the beef hot dog according to package instructions.
2. Place the hot dog in a bun.
3. Ladle a generous amount of Coney Island Chili Sauce over the hot dog.
4. Add diced onions and a drizzle of yellow mustard.
5. Sprinkle a generous amount of shredded cheddar cheese on top.
6. Savor the bold and comforting flavors of Detroit's culinary pride.

2 tacos | 300/ta co | 45 minutes

California Fish Tacos

A taste of the West Coast's vibrant culinary scene, California Fish Tacos are a refreshing fusion of flavors and textures. Crispy battered fish is nestled in soft tortillas and topped with slaw, salsa, and a squeeze of lime. This dish embodies the California spirit of fresh ingredients and culinary creativity. Savor the sunshine and coastal charm in each bite.

Ingredients:

- 1/2 lb white fish fillets (cod, tilapia, or mahi-mahi)
- 1/2 cup all-purpose flour
- 1/2 cup cornmeal
- 1 teaspoon paprika
- Salt and black pepper, to taste
- Vegetable oil, for frying
- 4 small flour tortillas
- Slaw mix (cabbage and carrot)
- Fresh salsa or pico de gallo
- Lime wedges, for serving
- Chopped fresh cilantro, for garnish

Substitutions

- Use corn tortillas for a gluten-free version or to enhance the authentic Mexican touch.
- Add sliced avocado, radishes, or pickled red onions for extra freshness and crunch.
- Serve with a side of Mexican street corn or black bean salad for a complete meal.
- Enjoy with a glass of chilled white wine or a citrusy IPA to complement the flavors.
- Listen to beach tunes or West Coast indie music while enjoying the tacos to fully embrace the California ambiance.

Directions

1. In a shallow dish, mix all-purpose flour, cornmeal, paprika, salt, and black pepper.
2. Coat the fish fillets in the flour mixture, shaking off excess.
3. Heat vegetable oil in a skillet over medium-high heat.
4. Fry the coated fish fillets until golden brown and cooked through.
5. Transfer the fish to a paper towel-lined plate to drain.
6. Warm the flour tortillas in a dry skillet or microwave.
7. Place a fried fish fillet in each tortilla.
8. Top with slaw mix, fresh salsa or pico de gallo, and a squeeze of lime.
9. Garnish with chopped fresh cilantro.
10. Let the flavors of the Pacific and the culinary creativity of California transport you to the coast with every bite.

8 wings

300/se rving

60 minutes

Buffalo Wings

Ingredients:

- 2 lbs chicken wings
- Salt and black pepper, to taste
- Vegetable oil, for frying
- 1/2 cup hot sauce (Frank's RedHot or your preferred brand)
- 1/4 cup unsalted butter, melted
- 1 tablespoon white vinegar
- Dash of Worcestershire sauce
- Dash of garlic powder
- Dash of cayenne pepper (adjust to taste)
- Blue cheese dressing, for dipping
- Celery sticks, for serving

Substitutions

- Adjust the level of cayenne pepper in the buffalo sauce to your preferred level of spiciness.
- Serve with a side of seasoned potato wedges or sweet potato fries for a satisfying meal.
- Enjoy with a cold beer or a creamy milkshake to balance the heat.
- Watch a sports game or host a wing-eating contest to fully embrace the Buffalo Wing experience.
- Listen to rock or energetic music while indulging in the wings to channel the sports bar ambiance.

A staple of sports bars and gatherings across the nation, Buffalo Wings are an American favorite that packs a punch of flavor. Crispy chicken wings are coated in tangy and spicy buffalo sauce, delivering a satisfying kick with every bite. Embrace the fiery spirit of these wings as you dive into their saucy goodness.

Directions

1. Preheat the oven to 425°F (220°C).
2. Season chicken wings with salt and black pepper.
3. Bake the wings on a baking sheet for about 45 minutes, turning once, until crispy and cooked through.
4. In a bowl, whisk together hot sauce, melted unsalted butter, white vinegar, Worcestershire sauce, garlic powder, and cayenne pepper.
5. Toss the baked wings in the buffalo sauce mixture to coat.
6. Heat vegetable oil in a deep skillet or pot to about 375°F (190°C).
7. Carefully place the coated wings in the hot oil and fry for about 2-3 minutes until crispy.
8. Remove from the oil and let drain on paper towels.
9. Serve the Buffalo Wings hot, accompanied by blue cheese dressing and celery sticks.
10. Let the fiery flavors and spirited goodness of Buffalo Wings ignite your taste buds.

2 peppers

350/pepper

75 minutes

Southwest Stuffed Bell Peppers

Ingredients:

- 2 large bell peppers (red, green, or yellow)
- 1/2 lb ground beef
- 1/2 cup cooked rice
- 1/2 cup cooked black beans
- 1/2 cup shredded cheese (cheddar or Mexican blend)
- 1/2 cup corn kernels (fresh, frozen, or canned)
- 1/4 cup diced tomatoes
- 1 teaspoon chili powder
- 1/2 teaspoon cumin
- Salt and black pepper, to taste
- Chopped fresh cilantro, for garnish
- Lime wedges, for serving

Substitutions

- Customize the filling with ground turkey, quinoa, or a mix of different beans for a healthier twist.
- Drizzle with a dollop of sour cream or a spoonful of salsa for added creaminess and zest.
- Serve with a side of tortilla chips or a green salad to round out the meal.
- Enjoy with a glass of cold iced tea or a tangy margarita to complement the Tex-Mex influence.
- Listen to country rock or southwestern music while savoring the stuffed peppers to fully embrace the fusion of flavors.

A fusion of flavors inspired by multiple states, Southwest Stuffed Bell Peppers take the classic comfort of stuffed peppers and infuse them with Tex-Mex flair. Stuffed with a mix of seasoned ground beef, rice, beans, and cheese, these peppers are a symphony of savory goodness. Enjoy the warmth of the Heartland with a southwestern twist.

Directions

1. Preheat the oven to 375°F (190°C).
2. Cut the tops off the bell peppers and remove the seeds and membranes.
3. In a skillet, cook ground beef until browned. Drain excess grease.
4. Stir in cooked rice, cooked black beans, shredded cheese, corn kernels, diced tomatoes, chili powder, cumin, salt, and black pepper.
5. Spoon the filling mixture into the hollowed bell peppers.
6. Place the stuffed peppers in a baking dish.
7. Cover the baking dish with aluminum foil and bake for about 35-40 minutes, until the peppers are tender.
8. Garnish with chopped fresh cilantro and serve with lime wedges.
9. Experience the fusion of Heartland comfort and Tex-Mex flavors in every satisfying bite.

1 hot dog

300/hot dog

30 minutes

Chicago-style Hot Dog

Ingredients:

- Beef hot dog
- Poppy seed hot dog bun
- Yellow mustard
- Sweet pickle relish
- Chopped onions
- Tomato slices
- Dill pickle spears
- Sport peppers
- Celery salt
- Dash of ground celery seed
- Dash of poppy seeds

Substitutions

- Adjust the toppings to your preference, omitting or adding ingredients as desired.
- Serve with a side of seasoned waffle fries or crispy onion rings for a satisfying crunch.
- Enjoy with a classic Chicago-made soda like Faygo or RC Cola for an authentic touch.
- Listen to jazz or blues music while enjoying your Chicago-style Hot Dog to fully embrace the Windy City vibe.

A true Windy City icon, the Chicago-style Hot Dog is a vibrant and flavorful creation that's both a feast for the eyes and the taste buds. Topped with a variety of ingredients including mustard, relish, onions, tomatoes, pickles, sport peppers, and celery salt, this hot dog is a culinary masterpiece that reflects Chicago's rich history and diversity. Let the layers of flavor transport you to the heart of the Midwest.

Directions

1. Steam or grill the beef hot dog until heated through and slightly browned.
2. Place the hot dog in a poppy seed hot dog bun.
3. Add a drizzle of yellow mustard and a layer of sweet pickle relish.
4. Sprinkle chopped onions over the relish.
5. Place tomato slices alongside the onions.
6. Nestle dill pickle spears and sport peppers into the toppings.
7. Generously sprinkle with celery salt, ground celery seed, and poppy seeds.
8. Experience the explosion of flavors that define Chicago's culinary masterpiece, the Chicago-style Hot Dog.

1 sandwich

450/sandwich

45 minutes

Kentucky Hot Brown Sandwich

Ingredients:

- 2 slices toasted bread (white or sourdough)
- 1/2 lb roasted turkey slices
- 4 slices cooked bacon
- 1 cup Mornay sauce (see Classic Macaroni and Cheese recipe)
- Tomato slices, for garnish
- Grated Pecorino Romano cheese, for garnish
- Paprika, for garnish

Substitutions

- Customize the sandwich with roasted chicken or ham for a variation on the classic recipe.
- Serve with a side of mixed greens or a classic Caesar salad to complement the richness.
- Pair with a glass of Kentucky bourbon or a refreshing mint julep for a true taste of the South.
- Listen to bluegrass or folk music while savoring the sandwich to fully embrace the Kentucky ambiance.

Hailing from the Bluegrass State, the Kentucky Hot Brown Sandwich is an open-faced masterpiece that combines layers of roasted turkey, crispy bacon, and a rich Mornay sauce. Baked to perfection and garnished with tomato slices and Pecorino Romano cheese, this sandwich is a taste of elegance and comfort in every bite. Savor the hospitality and refinement of Kentucky cuisine.

Directions

1. Preheat the oven broiler.
2. Place the toasted bread slices on a baking sheet.
3. Layer roasted turkey slices over the bread.
4. Arrange cooked bacon slices on top of the turkey.
5. Pour Mornay sauce over the sandwich, covering it completely.
6. Place the sandwich under the broiler for a few minutes until the sauce is bubbly and golden.
7. Garnish with tomato slices and a generous sprinkle of grated Pecorino Romano cheese.
8. Sprinkle paprika over the top for a burst of color and flavor.
9. Indulge in the refined flavors and elegant simplicity of Kentucky's Hot Brown Sandwich.

 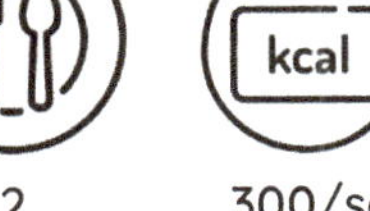 

2
scones

300/sc
one

60
minutes

Utah Scones

A unique delight from the Beehive State, Utah Scones are a cross between fried dough and scones. These soft and pillowy treats are fried until golden brown and can be enjoyed sweet or savory. Top with powdered sugar, honey, jam, or even chili for a versatile experience that captures Utah's creative and flavorful spirit. Embrace the culinary innovation with every bite.

Ingredients:

- 2 cups all-purpose flour
- 1 tablespoon sugar
- 1 teaspoon salt
- 2 teaspoons active dry yeast
- 1/2 cup warm water
- 1/4 cup milk
- 1 egg
- Vegetable oil, for frying
- Powdered sugar, for dusting
- Honey or jam, for topping (sweet option)
- Chili or cheese, for topping (savory option)

Substitutions

- Experiment with different toppings like Nutella, fruit compote, or whipped cream for a playful twist.
- Serve with a side of fresh fruit or a scoop of ice cream for an indulgent dessert.
- Enjoy with a glass of milk or a mug of hot cocoa for a comforting pairing.
- Listen to country tunes or folk music while savoring the scones to fully embrace the Utah ambiance.

Directions

1. In a bowl, mix all-purpose flour, sugar, and salt.
2. In a separate bowl, combine active dry yeast, warm water, and a pinch of sugar. Let it sit for about 5 minutes until foamy.
3. Mix milk and egg into the yeast mixture.
4. Gradually add the wet ingredients to the dry ingredients, stirring until a dough forms.
5. Cover the dough and let it rise in a warm place for about 30 minutes.
6. Heat vegetable oil in a skillet or pot to about 375°F (190°C).
7. Gently flatten a portion of the dough into a disc and fry it in the hot oil until puffed and golden brown on both sides.
8. Remove from the oil and let drain on paper towels.
9. Dust the Utah Scones with powdered sugar or top them with honey, jam, chili, or cheese, based on your preference.
10. Immerse yourself in the culinary innovation and creative spirit of Utah with each delectable bite.

Chapter 8:
Dessert Delights

1 slice

400/sli
ce

120
minutes

New York Cheesecake

Ingredients:

- 1 1/2 cups graham cracker crumbs
- 1/4 cup granulated sugar
- 1/2 cup unsalted butter, melted
- 4 packages (8 oz each) cream cheese, softened
- 1 cup granulated sugar
- 1 teaspoon vanilla extract
- 4 large eggs
- 1 cup sour cream
- 1/4 cup all-purpose flour
- Pinch of salt
- Fresh berries, for garnish
- Whipped cream, for topping

Directions

1. Preheat the oven to 325°F (160°C).
2. In a bowl, mix graham cracker crumbs, granulated sugar, and melted unsalted butter to create the crust mixture.
3. Press the crust mixture into the bottom of a springform pan to form an even layer.
4. In a mixing bowl, beat softened cream cheese, granulated sugar, and vanilla extract until smooth and creamy.
5. Add eggs one at a time, beating well after each addition.
6. Mix in sour cream, all-purpose flour, and a pinch of salt until fully incorporated.
7. Pour the cream cheese mixture over the crust in the pan.
8. Bake in the preheated oven for about 50-60 minutes, until the edges are set and the center is slightly jiggly.
9. Turn off the oven and leave the cheesecake inside for an additional hour.
10. Remove the cheesecake from the oven and let it cool completely before refrigerating for several hours or overnight.
11. Before serving, garnish with fresh berries and a dollop of whipped cream.
12. Savor the luxurious taste and timeless elegance of New York's iconic dessert.

1 slice

350/sli
ce

60
minutes

Mississippi Mud Pie

Ingredients:

- 1 1/2 cups chocolate cookie crumbs
- 1/4 cup unsalted butter, melted
- 1 package (8 oz) cream cheese, softened
- 1 cup powdered sugar
- 1 cup heavy whipping cream
- 1 cup semisweet chocolate chips, melted
- 1 teaspoon vanilla extract
- 3 cups whipped cream, for topping
- Chocolate shavings, for garnish

Substitutions

- Enhance the chocolate experience with a drizzle of warm chocolate ganache over the whipped cream topping.
- Sprinkle chopped nuts or mini marshmallows over the pie for added texture and flavor.
- Serve with a scoop of vanilla ice cream or a dollop of caramel sauce for extra decadence.
- Pair with a cup of strong coffee or a glass of sweet tea to round out the Southern experience.
- Listen to blues or Southern rock music while savoring the pie to fully embrace the Mississippi vibe.

Directions

1. In a bowl, mix chocolate cookie crumbs and melted unsalted butter to create the crust mixture.
2. Press the crust mixture into the bottom of a pie dish to form an even layer.
3. In a mixing bowl, beat softened cream cheese until smooth.
4. Gradually mix in powdered sugar until well combined.
5. In a separate bowl, whip heavy whipping cream until stiff peaks form.
6. Gently fold the whipped cream into the cream cheese mixture.
7. Add melted semisweet chocolate chips and vanilla extract, mixing until smooth.
8. Pour the chocolate filling over the crust in the pie dish.
9. Refrigerate the pie for several hours or until set.
10. Before serving, spread whipped cream over the top of the pie and garnish with chocolate shavings.
11. Immerse yourself in the deep and velvety flavors of Mississippi's dessert tradition.

1 slice

300/sli
ce

75
minutes

Oregon Marionberry Pie

Ingredients:

- 2 pre-made pie crusts (store-bought or homemade)
- 5 cups fresh or frozen marionberries
- 1 cup granulated sugar
- 1/4 cup cornstarch
- 1 tablespoon lemon juice
- Zest of 1 lemon
- Pinch of salt
- 1 egg, beaten (for egg wash)
- Turbinado sugar, for sprinkling

Substitutions

- Add a dash of cinnamon or nutmeg to the berry filling for a warm and aromatic twist.
- Serve with a scoop of vanilla ice cream or a dollop of whipped cream to enhance the sweetness.
- Pair with a glass of local Oregon wine or a refreshing berry-infused iced tea to complement the flavors.
- Listen to folk or indie music while enjoying your pie to fully embrace the Pacific Northwest ambiance.

Celebrate the bountiful flavors of the Pacific Northwest with Oregon Marionberry Pie. A buttery, flaky crust envelops a filling of ripe marionberries, a local treasure. With a touch of tanginess and sweetness, this pie captures the essence of Oregon's berry-rich landscapes. Delight in the taste of the Northwest with each juicy bite.

Directions

1. Preheat the oven to 375°F (190°C).
2. Line a pie dish with one of the pie crusts.
3. In a mixing bowl, gently toss marionberries with granulated sugar, cornstarch, lemon juice, lemon zest, and a pinch of salt.
4. Pour the berry mixture into the prepared pie crust.
5. Cover the pie with the second pie crust, sealing the edges and cutting slits for venting.
6. Brush the top crust with beaten egg and sprinkle with turbinado sugar.
7. Place the pie on a baking sheet to catch any drips.
8. Bake in the preheated oven for about 50-60 minutes, until the filling is bubbly and the crust is golden brown.
9. Let the pie cool before slicing and savoring the juicy goodness of Oregon's marionberries.

1 slice | 350/slice | 90 minutes

Deep Dish Apple Pie

Ingredients:

- 2 pre-made pie crusts (store-bought or homemade)
- 6-8 cups tart baking apples (Granny Smith, Honeycrisp, or similar), peeled, cored, and sliced
- 1 cup granulated sugar
- 1/4 cup all-purpose flour
- 1 teaspoon ground cinnamon
- 1/4 teaspoon ground nutmeg
- 1/4 teaspoon salt
- 2 tablespoons unsalted butter, diced
- 1 egg, beaten (for egg wash)
- Turbinado sugar, for sprinkling

Substitutions

- Add a handful of raisins or dried cranberries to the apple filling for a burst of sweetness and texture.
- Serve with a scoop of vanilla ice cream or a slice of sharp cheddar cheese for a classic pairing.
- Pair with a cup of warm spiced cider or a cozy cup of tea to complement the comforting flavors.
- Listen to folk tunes or timeless classics while enjoying your slice of pie to fully embrace the nostalgia.

Directions

1. Preheat the oven to 375°F (190°C).
2. Line a deep pie dish with one of the pie crusts.
3. In a mixing bowl, combine apple slices, granulated sugar, all-purpose flour, ground cinnamon, ground nutmeg, and salt. Toss until the apples are evenly coated.
4. Pour the apple mixture into the prepared pie crust, creating a mound in the center.
5. Dot the apples with diced unsalted butter.
6. Cover the pie with the second pie crust, crimping the edges to seal.
7. Brush the top crust with beaten egg and sprinkle with turbinado sugar.
8. Make slits in the top crust for venting.
9. Place the pie on a baking sheet to catch any drips.
10. Bake in the preheated oven for about 50-60 minutes, until the apples are tender and the crust is golden brown.
11. Allow the pie to cool before slicing and savoring the heartwarming taste of Deep Dish Apple Pie.

1
serving

300/se
rving

60
minutes

Peach Cobbler

Ingredients:

- 4 cups peeled and sliced peaches (fresh, frozen, or canned)
- 1 cup granulated sugar
- 1/2 teaspoon ground cinnamon
- 1/4 teaspoon salt
- 1 cup all-purpose flour
- 2 teaspoons baking powder
- 1/2 teaspoon salt
- 1 cup milk
- 1/2 cup unsalted butter, melted
- Whipped cream or vanilla ice cream, for serving

Substitutions

- Add a sprinkle of nutmeg or a splash of vanilla extract to the peach mixture for extra depth of flavor.
- Serve with a drizzle of honey or a sprinkle of powdered sugar for added sweetness.
- Pair with a glass of sweet tea or a mason jar of fresh lemonade to complete the Southern experience.
- Listen to country tunes or soulful ballads while enjoying your cobbler to fully embrace the Southern ambiance.

A beloved Southern treat, Peach Cobbler is a celebration of ripe peaches nestled beneath a tender biscuit crust. With a touch of cinnamon and a dollop of whipped cream, this dessert captures the essence of hospitality and comfort. Let the warm flavors transport you to a porch swing in the heart of the South.

Directions

1. Preheat the oven to 375°F (190°C).
2. In a mixing bowl, combine sliced peaches, granulated sugar, ground cinnamon, and a pinch of salt. Toss until the peaches are coated.
3. Spread the peach mixture evenly in a baking dish.
4. In another bowl, whisk all-purpose flour, baking powder, and salt.
5. Stir in milk and melted unsalted butter to create the batter.
6. Pour the batter over the peaches, spreading it gently.
7. Bake in the preheated oven for about 45-50 minutes, until the top is golden brown and the cobbler is bubbly.
8. Allow the cobbler to cool slightly before serving with whipped cream or vanilla ice cream.
9. Let the flavors of the South warm your heart with each delightful spoonful of Peach Cobbler.

1 slice | 320/slice | 45 minutes

Key Lime Pie

Transport yourself to the Florida Keys with Key Lime Pie, a tangy and refreshing dessert with a sweet and zesty filling made from key lime juice. Set in a buttery graham cracker crust and topped with whipped cream, this pie captures the essence of the tropics in each citrusy bite. Savor the sunshine and sea breeze with this delightful treat.

Ingredients:

- 1 1/2 cups graham cracker crumbs
- 1/4 cup granulated sugar
- 1/2 cup unsalted butter, melted
- 3/4 cup key lime juice
- 1 can (14 oz) sweetened condensed milk
- 3 large egg yolks
- Zest of 2 limes
- Whipped cream, for topping

Substitutions

- Add a splash of coconut milk or a sprinkle of toasted coconut flakes to the filling for a tropical twist.
- Serve with a slice of lime or a drizzle of raspberry sauce for an extra burst of flavor and color.
- Pair with a glass of tangy lemonade or a refreshing mojito to complement the zesty profile.
- Listen to reggae or tropical tunes while enjoying your slice of pie to fully embrace the Key West vibes.

Directions

1. Preheat the oven to 350°F (175°C).
2. In a bowl, mix graham cracker crumbs, granulated sugar, and melted unsalted butter to create the crust mixture.
3. Press the crust mixture into the bottom of a pie dish to form an even layer.
4. In another bowl, whisk together key lime juice, sweetened condensed milk, egg yolks, and lime zest until well combined.
5. Pour the key lime filling into the prepared crust.
6. Bake in the preheated oven for about 15-20 minutes, until the filling is set but still slightly jiggly.
7. Let the pie cool to room temperature before refrigerating for several hours or until fully chilled.
8. Before serving, garnish with a generous dollop of whipped cream.
9. Embrace the tropical zest and sunny flavors of Florida's Key Lime Pie with every citrus-infused bite.

2
tablesp
oons

100/2
tbsp

10
minutes

Vermont Maple Syrup

Ingredients:

- 100% pure Vermont maple syrup

Substitutions

- Experiment with different grades of maple syrup, from light to dark, to explore varying levels of flavor intensity.
- Use maple syrup as a glaze for roasted meats or vegetables for a delightful caramelized finish.
- Mix maple syrup into cocktails or mocktails for a hint of sweetness and complexity.
- Listen to folk music or nature sounds while enjoying your maple syrup-infused creations to fully embrace the Vermont experience.

Straight from the maple trees of the Green Mountain State, Vermont Maple Syrup is liquid gold that adds sweetness and depth to a variety of dishes. Drizzle it over pancakes, waffles, yogurt, or even bacon for a touch of natural indulgence. Let the rich flavors of Vermont elevate your breakfast and beyond.

Directions

1. Warm the Vermont Maple Syrup by placing the bottle in a bowl of hot water or microwaving it for a few seconds.
2. Drizzle the warm maple syrup over your favorite breakfast dishes, whether it's pancakes, waffles, or yogurt.
3. For a savory-sweet twist, try adding a touch of maple syrup to cooked bacon or sautéed vegetables.
4. Embrace the natural sweetness of Vermont's finest maple trees and enjoy the rich flavors that elevate every bite.

1 slice | 320/slice | 75 minutes

Huckleberry Pie

Ingredients:

- 2 pre-made pie crusts (store-bought or homemade)
- 4 cups fresh huckleberries (or frozen)
- 1 cup granulated sugar
- 1/4 cup cornstarch
- 1 tablespoon lemon juice
- Zest of 1 lemon
- Pinch of salt
- 1 egg, beaten (for egg wash)
- Turbinado sugar, for sprinkling

Substitutions

- Combine huckleberries with other berries like blueberries or raspberries for a mixed berry pie.
- Serve with a scoop of vanilla ice cream or a dollop of whipped cream to enhance the sweetness.
- Pair with a glass of local Montana wine or a mug of herbal tea to complement the natural flavors.
- Listen to folk tunes or sounds of nature while enjoying your slice of pie to fully embrace the Montana wilderness.

Bursting with the flavors of the Rocky Mountains, Huckleberry Pie showcases the wild huckleberries found in the rugged landscapes of Montana. With a sweet-tart filling nestled in a flaky crust, this pie is a true taste of the great outdoors. Immerse yourself in the natural beauty and vibrant flavors of Montana with each berry-filled bite.

Directions

1. Preheat the oven to 375°F (190°C).
2. Line a pie dish with one of the pie crusts.
3. In a mixing bowl, gently toss huckleberries with granulated sugar, cornstarch, lemon juice, lemon zest, and a pinch of salt.
4. Pour the berry mixture into the prepared pie crust.
5. Cover the pie with the second pie crust, crimping the edges to seal.
6. Brush the top crust with beaten egg and sprinkle with turbinado sugar.
7. Make slits in the top crust for venting.
8. Place the pie on a baking sheet to catch any drips.
9. Bake in the preheated oven for about 50-60 minutes, until the filling is bubbly and the crust is golden brown.
10. Allow the pie to cool before slicing and savoring the wild and vibrant flavors of Montana's Huckleberry Pie.

1 slice | 400/slice | 75 minutes

Texas Pecan Pie

A Southern favorite with a Texan twist, Texas Pecan Pie is a nutty and caramel-filled delight that embodies the Lone Star State's hospitality. With a buttery crust and a filling of pecans, sugar, and corn syrup, this pie is a sweet celebration of Texas flavors. Indulge in the warmth and charm of the South with each pecan-packed bite.

Ingredients:

- 1 pre-made pie crust (store-bought or homemade)
- 1 1/2 cups pecan halves
- 1 cup granulated sugar
- 1 cup light corn syrup
- 4 large eggs
- 1/4 cup unsalted butter, melted
- 1 teaspoon vanilla extract
- 1/4 teaspoon salt
- Whipped cream or vanilla ice cream, for serving

Substitutions

- Add a sprinkle of cinnamon or a dash of bourbon to the filling for an extra layer of flavor.
- Serve with a drizzle of caramel sauce or a dusting of powdered sugar for added indulgence.
- Pair with a cup of strong coffee or a glass of sweet tea to complement the richness of the pie.
- Listen to country tunes or classic rock while enjoying your slice of pie to fully embrace the Texan spirit.

Directions

1. Preheat the oven to 350°F (175°C).
2. Line a pie dish with the pre-made pie crust.
3. Arrange pecan halves in the pie crust in an even layer.
4. In a mixing bowl, whisk granulated sugar, light corn syrup, eggs, melted unsalted butter, vanilla extract, and salt until well combined.
5. Pour the sugar mixture over the pecans in the pie crust.
6. Bake in the preheated oven for about 50-60 minutes, until the filling is set and slightly puffed.
7. Allow the pie to cool before slicing and serving with whipped cream or vanilla ice cream.
8. Experience the nutty richness and Southern sweetness of Texas Pecan Pie with every delectable bite.

1 slice

280/sli
ce

60
minutes

Hawaiian Pineapple Upside-Down Cake

Ingredients:

- 1/4 cup unsalted butter
- 2/3 cup packed brown sugar
- 7-8 canned pineapple rings, drained
- Maraschino cherries, drained and patted dry
- 1 1/2 cups all-purpose flour
- 1 cup granulated sugar
- 1 1/2 teaspoons baking powder
- 1/2 teaspoon salt
- 1/2 cup unsalted butter, softened
- 1/2 cup milk
- 2 large eggs
- 1 teaspoon vanilla extract
- Whipped cream or vanilla ice cream, for serving
- Toasted coconut flakes, for garnish

Directions

1. Preheat the oven to 350°F (175°C).
2. In a saucepan, melt 1/4 cup unsalted butter over medium heat.
3. Stir in packed brown sugar until melted and smooth.
4. Pour the butter-sugar mixture into the bottom of a round cake pan, spreading it evenly.
5. Arrange pineapple rings and maraschino cherries in the bottom of the pan.
6. In a mixing bowl, whisk all-purpose flour, granulated sugar, baking powder, and salt.
7. Add softened unsalted butter and milk, mixing until smooth.
8. Mix in eggs and vanilla extract until well combined.
9. Pour the batter over the pineapple and cherries in the cake pan.
10. Bake in the preheated oven for about 30-35 minutes, until the cake is golden brown and a toothpick inserted into the center comes out clean.
11. Allow the cake to cool for a few minutes before inverting it onto a serving platter.
12. Serve warm with whipped cream or vanilla ice cream, and garnish with toasted coconut flakes.
13. Let the tropical flavors of Hawaii transport you to paradise with every luscious bite of Pineapple Upside-Down Cake.

Chapter 9:
Unique Eats

1 pretzel   350   20

Philly Soft Pretzel

Ingredients:

- 1 packet active dry yeast
- 1 ½ cups warm water
- 1 tsp salt
- 1 tsp sugar
- 4 cups all-purpose flour
- Cooking spray
- ½ cup baking soda
- Coarse salt, for topping

Note: Some extra flour might be needed for dusting.

A twist of doughy magic from Philadelphia's streets. Legend has it, German immigrants shaped these treats to resemble the German Flag. They're loved for their chewy crust and fluffy insides.

Directions

1. In a bowl, dissolve yeast in warm water. Add sugar and salt.
2. Stir in flour gradually to form a dough.
3. Knead dough on a floured surface until smooth. Rest for 10 min.
4. Divide into sections and roll to form ropes, shape into pretzels.
5. Boil water, add baking soda.
6. Boil pretzels, then bake after draining.
7. Sprinkle salt and enjoy warm.

10 pieces

280

25

St. Louis Toasted Ravioli

Ingredients:

- 1 package meat ravioli
- 2 eggs
- 2 tbsp milk
- 2 cups breadcrumbs
- 1 cup grated parmesan cheese
- 1 tsp dried oregano
- 1 tsp garlic powder
- Salt and pepper to taste
- Marinara sauce, for dipping

A crunchy revelation from Missouri's Italian-American community. As the story goes, ravioli accidentally met breadcrumbs and hot oil. Now it's a staple appetizer loved for its texture and taste.

Directions

1. Whisk eggs and milk in a bowl.
2. Mix breadcrumbs, parmesan, oregano, garlic powder, salt & pepper.
3. Dip ravioli in egg mixture, coat with breadcrumb mixture.
4. Arrange on baking sheet, refrigerate for 20 min.
5. Bake until golden and crisp.
6. Serve with warm marinara sauce.

6 balls   210   40

Cajun Boudin Balls

Ingredients:

- 1 cup cooked boudin sausage
- 2 cups cooked rice
- 2 eggs
- 1 cup breadcrumbs
- 1 tsp Cajun seasoning
- Vegetable oil for frying

A spicy delight cherished in the heart of Louisiana. Born from frugality, boudin balls use leftover pork and rice. Spices give them a Cajun kick. Perfect for sharing, or not!

Directions

1. Remove boudin from casings, mix with rice.
2. Form mixture into golf-sized balls.
3. Beat eggs in one bowl, place breadcrumbs in another.
4. Dip balls in egg, then coat with breadcrumbs.
5. Heat oil to 350°F, fry until golden.
6. Drain on paper towels, sprinkle with Cajun seasoning.

1 slice   180   45

Cincinnati Goetta

Ingredients:

- 1 lb ground pork
- 1 lb ground beef
- 1 cup steel-cut oats
- 5 cups water
- 1 onion, finely chopped
- 1 tsp salt
- ½ tsp black pepper
- ½ tsp ground cloves
- ½ tsp ground nutmeg

An Ohioan favorite born out of thriftiness. Goetta brings together ground meat, oats, and spices. Sliced and fried, it's comfort food with a crispy twist.

Directions

1. Combine meat, oats, water, onion, and spices in a pot.
2. Cook on low, stirring occasionally, for 3 hours.
3. Pour into loaf pans, refrigerate until firm.
4. Slice and fry in butter until crispy.
5. Serve with mustard or maple syrup.

1 burger

550

30

Wisconsin Butter Burger

Ingredients:

- 1/2 lb ground beef
- Salt and pepper to taste
- 1 hamburger bun
- 2 tbsp unsalted butter
- Cheese slices (cheddar or American)
- Lettuce, tomato, onions, pickles for toppings

Wisconsin's answer to burger cravings. A juicy patty is cooked in butter until caramelized. Topped with cheese and condiments, it's a decadent delight.

Directions

1. Season beef with salt and pepper, shape into patty.
2. Heat a skillet, melt 1 tbsp butter.
3. Cook patty in butter until desired doneness.
4. Butter and toast bun in skillet.
5. Place cheese on patty to melt.
6. Assémble with toppings, enjoy the buttery goodness.

1 slice | 320 | 50

Oregon Marionberry Pie

Ingredients:

- 4 cups fresh or frozen marionberries
- 1 cup granulated sugar
- 1/4 cup cornstarch
- 1 tbsp lemon juice
- 2 prepared pie crusts
- 1 tbsp butter (for dotting)

A sweet treasure from Oregon's berry-laden fields. Marionberries, a cross between blackberries and raspberries, shine in this pie. Their natural tartness pairs perfectly with a flaky crust.

Directions

1. Preheat oven to 375°F.
2. Mix marionberries, sugar, cornstarch, and lemon juice.
3. Place one pie crust in pan, add filling.
4. Dot filling with butter, cover with second crust.
5. Seal and vent the top crust, trim excess.
6. Bake until golden and bubbly, about 45 minutes.
7. Cool before slicing and serving.

1 slice   420   40

Arkansas Possum Pie

Ingredients:

- 1 ½ cups graham cracker crumbs
- 1/4 cup granulated sugar
- 1/2 cup unsalted butter, melted
- 8 oz cream cheese, softened
- 1 cup powdered sugar
- 1 cup whipped cream
- 2 small boxes chocolate pudding
- Chopped nuts, chocolate shavings for garnish

A quirky yet delicious dessert born in Arkansas. Despite the name, it's possum-free! Layers of cream cheese, chocolate pudding, and whipped cream mingle for a heavenly treat.

Directions

1. Mix graham cracker crumbs, sugar, and melted butter.
2. Press into pie pan, bake at 350°F for 10 min, cool.
3. Beat cream cheese and powdered sugar until smooth, spread over crust.
4. Prepare chocolate pudding, layer over cream cheese.
5. Spread whipped cream on top, garnish with nuts and chocolate shavings.
6. Chill before serving and delight in layers of goodness.

1 slice   280   60

Michigan Cherry Pie

Ingredients:

- 4 cups pitted cherries (mix of sweet and tart)
- 1 cup granulated sugar
- 1/4 cup cornstarch
- 1/4 tsp almond extract
- 2 prepared pie crusts
- 1 tbsp unsalted butter (for dotting)

A fruity marvel that captures the essence of Michigan. Juicy cherries, both sweet and tart, burst within a flaky crust. This pie embodies summer in every bite.

Directions

1. Preheat oven to 425°F.
2. Mix cherries, sugar, cornstarch, and almond extract.
3. Place one pie crust in pan, add filling.
4. Dot filling with butter, cover with second crust.
5. Seal and vent the top crust, trim excess.
6. Bake for 45-50 minutes, until golden and filling is bubbly.
7. Let cool slightly before slicing into the essence of Michigan.

1 hot dog

380

15

Arizona Sonoran Hot Dog

Ingredients:

- 1 bacon-wrapped hot dog
- 1 bolillo roll or hot dog bun
- 1/4 cup pinto beans, cooked and mashed
- 2 tbsp diced onion
- 2 tbsp diced tomatoes
- 1 tbsp diced roasted green chilies
- 1 tbsp mayonnaise
- 1 tbsp mustard
- 1 tbsp ketchup
- 1 tbsp Cotija cheese (optional)

A taste of the southwest wrapped in a bun. A bacon-wrapped hot dog is grilled to perfection and loaded with a medley of toppings, including beans, onions, and peppers.

Directions

1. Grill or cook bacon-wrapped hot dog until crispy and cooked through.
2. Toast roll/bun on grill or in a skillet.
3. Spread mashed beans on one side of the bun.
4. Place the cooked hot dog on the beans.
5. Layer with diced onion, tomatoes, and green chilies.
6. Drizzle with mayo, mustard, and ketchup.
7. Sprinkle Cotija cheese if desired.
8. Wrap your taste buds in a Southwest hug as you enjoy.

1 scoop 220 40

Utah Funeral Potatoes

A comforting casserole that's a staple at gatherings in Utah. With potatoes as the star, this dish is a hearty blend of creamy, cheesy, and crunchy goodness.

Ingredients:

- 4 cups frozen shredded hash browns
- 1/2 cup unsalted butter, melted
- 1 can condensed cream of chicken soup
- 2 cups sour cream
- 2 cups shredded cheddar cheese
- 1 cup crushed cornflakes
- Salt and pepper to taste

Directions

1. Preheat oven to 350°F.
2. In a bowl, combine hash browns and melted butter.
3. Mix in cream of chicken soup, sour cream, and shredded cheese.
4. Season with salt and pepper.
5. Spread mixture in a baking dish.
6. Top with crushed cornflakes for crunch.
7. Bake for 45 minutes until bubbly and golden.
8. Serve this warm, comforting embrace of a dish.

Chapter 10:
Homestyle Favorites

1 roll   290   90

West Virginia Pepperoni Roll

Ingredients:

- 1 lb pizza dough
- 1 cup sliced pepperoni
- 2 cups shredded mozzarella cheese
- Olive oil, for brushing

A savory marvel born in West Virginia's coal mines. Miners needed a hearty, portable meal. A soft roll embraces pepperoni, creating a handheld delight enjoyed by all.

Directions

1. Preheat oven to 375°F.
2. Roll out dough, layer with pepperoni and cheese.
3. Roll up tightly, pinching edges to seal.
4. Brush with olive oil, sprinkle with garlic powder.
5. Bake for 25-30 min, until golden.
6. Let cool slightly before savoring a taste of West Virginia history.

1 steak | 420 | 40

Oklahoma Chicken Fried Steak

Ingredients:

- 4 beef cube steaks
- Salt and pepper to taste
- 1 cup all-purpose flour
- 2 eggs
- 1 cup milk
- 1 cup breadcrumbs
- 1/4 cup vegetable oil

A hearty dish that's the pride of Oklahoma. Tenderized steak is coated, fried until golden, and served with creamy gravy. It's comfort food that's hard to resist.

Directions

1. Season steaks with salt and pepper.
2. Dredge steaks in flour.
3. Beat eggs and milk in one bowl.
4. Dip floured steaks in egg mixture, then coat with breadcrumbs.
5. Heat oil in skillet, fry steaks until golden on both sides.
6. Drain on paper towels.
7. Serve with creamy gravy and a side of comfort.

1 plate   600   30

Hawaii Loco Moco

Ingredients:

- 1/2 lb ground beef
- Salt and pepper to taste
- 2 cups cooked white rice
- 1 sunny-side-up egg
- 1 cup beef gravy
- Chopped green onions, for garnish

A Hawaiian creation that's pure indulgence. This dish stacks white rice, a juicy hamburger patty, a sunny-side-up egg, and rich gravy. It's a hearty and satisfying meal.

Directions

1. Season beef with salt and pepper, shape into patty.
2. Cook patty to desired doneness.
3. Prepare rice and egg.
4. Assemble by placing rice on plate, followed by patty and egg.
5. Pour gravy over the patty.
6. Garnish with chopped green onions.
7. Indulge in the Hawaiian comfort and flavors.

1
kolache

280

120

Texas Kolache

Ingredients:

- 3 cups all-purpose flour
- 1/4 cup granulated sugar
- 1 packet active dry yeast
- 1 cup milk
- 1/4 cup unsalted butter, melted
- 1/2 tsp salt
- 1 egg
- Filling of choice (sausage, cheese, fruit preserves)

A Texan treat that's both sweet and savory. Originating from Czech immigrants, these pastries are filled with various fillings like sausage, cheese, or fruit. They're a delight for any time of day.

Directions

1. In a bowl, mix 1 cup flour, sugar, and yeast.
2. Heat milk until warm, add to flour mixture along with melted butter.
3. Mix in salt, egg, and remaining flour to form a soft dough.
4. Knead until smooth, then cover and let rise until doubled.
5. Punch down dough and divide into portions.
6. Flatten each portion and place filling in the center, then fold and seal.
7. Let rise again for 15 min, then bake at 375°F for 12-15 min.
8. Enjoy these Texan delights, perfect for any craving.

1 brat   350   40

Wisconsin Beer Brats

Ingredients:

- 6 bratwurst sausages
- 2 cups beer (pilsner or lager)
- 1 onion, sliced
- 6 bratwurst buns
- Mustard and sauerkraut for topping

A Wisconsin tradition that's flavorful and fun. Bratwurst sausages are simmered in beer and onions, then grilled to perfection. They're a must-have at summer cookouts.

Directions

1. In a skillet, combine beer and sliced onions, bring to a simmer.
2. Add bratwurst sausages to the skillet, simmer for 15-20 min.
3. Preheat grill to medium-high heat.
4. Grill brats for 5-7 min, turning occasionally, until nicely browned.
5. Serve brats in buns, topped with mustard and sauerkraut.
6. Experience the Wisconsin tradition with every juicy bite.

1
serving

320

60

Georgia Peach Cobbler

Ingredients:

- 4 cups sliced peeled peaches
- 1 cup granulated sugar
- 1/2 cup unsalted butter
- 1 cup all-purpose flour
- 1 tbsp baking powder
- 1/4 tsp salt
- 1 cup milk

A Southern classic that's the epitome of comfort. Sweet, juicy peaches are baked beneath a layer of buttery, biscuit-like topping. It's warm, inviting, and full of flavor.

Directions

1. Preheat oven to 375°F.
2. In a saucepan, combine peaches and sugar, bring to a boil, then simmer.
3. Melt butter in a baking dish.
4. In a bowl, mix flour, baking powder, salt, and milk to form batter.
5. Pour batter over melted butter, then spoon peaches over batter.
6. Bake for 45-50 min until topping is golden and bubbly.
7. Serve warm, embracing the comforting taste of Georgia.

1 glass   120   5

Rhode Island Coffee Milk

Ingredients:

- 1 cup cold milk
- 2 tbsp coffee syrup

A simple delight that's Rhode Island's official state drink. Cold milk meets sweet coffee syrup for a refreshing and nostalgic beverage. It's a sip of New England charm.

Directions

1. Pour cold milk into a glass.
2. Add coffee syrup and stir well.
3. Adjust the amount of syrup to taste.
4. Sip and savor the sweet essence of Rhode Island.

1 slice   380   60

Indiana Sugar Cream Pie

Ingredients:

- 1 pie crust (store-bought or homemade)
- 1 cup granulated sugar
- 1/2 cup all-purpose flour
- 1/2 tsp ground nutmeg
- 1/4 tsp salt
- 1 1/2 cups heavy cream
- 1/2 cup milk
- 2 tbsp unsalted butter

A pie that's rich in history and flavor. Also known as Hoosier Pie, it boasts a velvety custard filling with a hint of nutmeg, all nestled in a flaky crust.

Directions

1. Preheat oven to 350°F.
2. Line pie crust in a pie pan.
3. Mix sugar, flour, nutmeg, and salt in a bowl.
4. Add heavy cream, milk, and butter to a pot, bring to a simmer.
5. Gradually whisk in the dry ingredients, cook until thickened.
6. Pour filling into the crust.
7. Bake for 40-45 min until filling is set and crust is golden.
8. Let cool before slicing into a piece of Indiana's heritage.

1
serving

280

50

Washington Apple Crisp

A dessert that celebrates Washington's bounty. Sliced apples are baked with a crispy oat topping, resulting in a warm and comforting treat that's best enjoyed with a scoop of vanilla ice cream.

Ingredients:

- 4 cups sliced and peeled apples
- 1/2 cup granulated sugar
- 1 tbsp lemon juice
- 1/2 tsp ground cinnamon
- 1/2 cup old-fashioned oats
- 1/4 cup all-purpose flour
- 1/4 cup brown sugar
- 1/4 cup unsalted butter, melted
- Vanilla ice cream for serving

Directions

1. Preheat oven to 350°F.
2. Toss sliced apples with granulated sugar, lemon juice, and cinnamon.
3. Spread apples in a baking dish.
4. In a bowl, combine oats, flour, brown sugar, and melted butter.
5. Crumble oat mixture over apples.
6. Bake for 30-35 min until topping is golden and apples are tender.
7. Serve warm with a scoop of vanilla ice cream.
8. Savor the taste of Washington's orchards in every bite.

Substitutions

-

1 slice | 420 | 60

Alabama Lane Cake

Ingredients:

- 2 1/2 cups all-purpose flour
- 2 1/2 tsp baking powder
- 1/2 tsp salt
- 1 cup unsalted butter, softened
- 2 cups granulated sugar
- 4 large eggs
- 1 cup whole milk
- 1 tsp vanilla extract
- 1/2 cup raisins
- 1/2 cup chopped pecans
- 1/4 cup whiskey
- 1/4 cup shredded coconut

A cake with a story, deeply rooted in Alabama's traditions. Layered with raisins, pecans, and a rich filling of whiskey and coconut, this cake is a cherished dessert with a touch of history.

Directions

1. Preheat oven to 350°F.
2. In a bowl, mix flour, baking powder, and salt.
3. In another bowl, cream butter and sugar until light and fluffy.
4. Beat in eggs, one at a time.
5. Gradually add flour mixture, alternating with milk and vanilla.
6. Fold in raisins and pecans.
7. Pour batter into greased and floured cake pans, bake for 25-30 min.
8. While the cakes cool, prepare the whiskey-coconut filling.
9. Spread filling between cake layers, then frost the cake.
10. Garnish with shredded coconut and a sprinkle of history.

We need your support

As we reach the end of this book, we want to express our heartfelt appreciation for joining us on this culinary journey. Before you close this chapter, we have a humble request.

Reviews are a rare treasure for us, especially as a small publisher. If you could spare a moment, we kindly ask you to return to the app or platform where you made your purchase. There, you'll find the review button. We would be immensely grateful if you could leave a rating and a brief sentence about your experience with the book.

These reviews hold immense value for us and can significantly impact our efforts to bring more delicious recipes to you. Every review is cherished and read with care.

Additionally, if you happen to notice any minor mistakes, please know that we've done our utmost to ensure a seamless experience. However, errors can occasionally slip through the cracks, and we hope you can overlook them.

Once again, thank you for your support, and we hope you continue to enjoy the culinary delights within these pages.